Management for Professionals

The Springer series *Management for Professionals* comprises high-level business and management books for executives. The authors are experienced business professionals and renowned professors who combine scientific background, best practice, and entrepreneurial vision to provide powerful insights into how to achieve business excellence.

More information about this series at http://www.springer.com/series/10101

Marc Helmold

Lean Management and Kaizen

Fundamentals from Cases and Examples in Operations and Supply Chain Management

Springer

Marc Helmold
IUBH International University
Berlin, Germany

ISSN 2192-8096 ISSN 2192-810X (electronic)
Management for Professionals
ISBN 978-3-030-46980-1 ISBN 978-3-030-46981-8 (eBook)
https://doi.org/10.1007/978-3-030-46981-8

This Springer imprint is published by the registered company Springer Nature Switzerland AG
The registered company address is: Gewerbestrasse 11, 6330 Cham, Switzerland

Fall down seven times, get up eight
Japanese Proverb
Unknown Author

Acknowledgements

The increasing (especially the digital) interconnection and the unlimited exchange of data and information has led to a maximised transparency of value adding activities and global supply chains. This is leading to the question how to generate a competitive advantage for companies in the producing, trading, service or healthcare industries.

In this context and as a consequence, there is a paradigm shift nowadays to manage the value chain from the supply side over the entire production towards the customers. Only the integrative approach from the customer order, planning, procurement, production and logistics up to the reverse logistics process will enable enterprises to make decisions for the management of their business actions. Moreover, due to the concentration on core competencies and the allocation of value adding non-core activities (outsourcing) to supply networks, new processes and flows are created that need to be coped with. Lean Management is the ideal way to concentrate on processes and activities, for which the customer is willing to pay.

Even though the concept of Lean Management is not new, companies understand that the implementation of this framework will lead to significant improvements in all areas from raw material suppliers to the end customers. Lean Management is no longer focusing on the own operations activities but is managing the exchange of information and the exploitation of advantages across global supply and value-adding chains. What opportunities are evolving to differentiate against competitors in the future? What are the customers´ expectations in terms of demanded products alongside the traditional requirements of price, quality and delivery? What are additional value adding activities and services within the supply chain to differentiate? Gradually declining factor advantages like increasing wages, volatile exchange rate parities, and yet challenging logistics chains necessitate more sophisticated and complimentary levers to further optimise cost alongside the value chain.

The basis for the next step and the Lean Management Vision 2030 is already set: On the one hand, the rising interconnection and automation generate the necessary process optimisations, on the other hand this trend leads to reduced labour intensive and manual production, which elevates the integration of all supply chain partners. The future challenges to obtain a competitive advantage lead to a new Lean Management concept of creating and managing value adding supply networks over the entire value chain. Thus, it will be possible to satisfy more and more demanding customers in increasingly transparent and open markets. In this context, newly internet-based information and communication strategies and concepts will be the ideal conjunction of stakeholders´ interest within the entire value chain. Pioneering companies like Tesla, Porsche, Alibaba and Amazon set the new benchmarks and meet the customer expectations in terms of growing expectations of lead times and availability of products.

Prof. Helmold had several top management positions in leading companies in Germany, the Czech Republic, Japan and China. Currently, He teaches performance management, supply chain management and negotiations in the international context at the IUBH University in Berlin and other universities in the UK and China. He also supports companies in supply, performance or project management.

The book would not have been possible without the implicit and indirect support of practitioners, academics and students on doctoral and master levels. For the practical relevance, the authors appreciate the input from professionals in many industries and from public organisations. Additionally, many of the impulses come from students of the IUBH university campus studies in Berlin. The author hopes that the book will also contribute to understand other countries and cultures in a better way, as he is convinced that diversity and intercultural experience in enterprises is a key success factor in a highly competitive environment. We would like to thank our colleagues, students and friends for giving us the impulse to write this book with many USPs.

Berlin, Shanghai and Tokyo, January 2020 Marc Helmold

Contents

List of Acronyms and Abbreviations

AI	Artificial Intelligence
AM	Additive Manufacturing
AR	Augmented Reality
BME	Bundesverband Materialwirtschaft, Einkauf und Logistik
BMW	Bayerische Motorenwerke
BOS	Bombardier Operating System
BSC	Balanced Score Card
CSR	Corporate Social Responsibility
DIN	Deutsche Industrienorm
DSCM	Downstream Supply Chain Management
ERP	Enterprise Resource Planning
EXW	Ex works
IOP	Internet of People
IoT	Internet of Things
IPO	International Procurement Office
ISO	International Standardisation Organisation
IUBH	International University Bad Honnef
JIT	Just-in-Time
KPI	Key Performance Indicator
MPS	Mercedes Benz Production System
OEE	Overall Equipment Effectiveness
OKR	Objectives Key Results
PDCA	Plan, Do, Check, Act
PDSA	Plan, Do, Study, Act
PE	Physical Education
PESTEL	Macro Analysis
PPS	Production Planning System
QR	Quick Response
SCM	Supply Chain Management
SFM	Shop floor Management
TIMWOOD	Seven Types of Waste in Manufacturing
TÜV	Technischer Überwachungsverein
UN	United Nations
USCM	Upstream Supply Chain Management

USP	Unique Selling Propositions
VW	Volkswagen
5S	Seiri, Seiton, Seiso, Seiketsu, Shitsuke
7R	7 Rights

List of Figures

List of Tables

About the Author

Marc Helmold (M.B.A.) is Professor at IUBH Internationale Hochschule in Berlin. He teaches Performance Management, Lean Management, Procurement, General Management, Strategic Management and Supply Chain Management to bachelor's and master's degree students as well as M.B.A. students.

From 1997 until 2017, he had several positions in top management positions in the automotive and railway industry. Between 1997 and 2010, he worked in several companies like Ford, Ford-Mazda Japan, Porsche and Panasonic Automotive in managerial functions and executed lean workshops throughout the value chain.

From 2013 until 2016, he was the General Manager of Bombardier Transportation in China and led the sourcing and spare parts sales activities. Since 2016, he is Professor at the IUBH and has his own consultancy. In this capacity, he improves performance of companies.

Basics in Lean Management

1

The Toyota style is not to create results by working hard. It is a system that says there is no limit to people's creativity. People don't go to Toyota to "work" they go there to "think".

Taiichi Ohno (1912–1990)

1.1 Definition of Lean Management

Lean management is a modern concept for process optimization throughout the value chain (Helmold and Samara 2019). Lean management is focusing on making inefficiencies (waste) transparent and on altering these into value-adding activities (Ohno 1990; Helmold and Terry 2016). The value chain reaches in this context from the upstream (suppliers) over the own operations to the downstream side (customers) (Slack et al. 1995). Inefficiencies are everything, e.g. an activity, a process, and a product, which is considered as something for which the customers are not willing to pay for or to spend financial means. The customer is the central point in the lean management concept. The primary objectives in the lean management philosophy are to create value for the customer through the optimization of resources and create a steady workflow based on real customer demands (Ohno 1990). It seeks to eliminate any waste of time, effort, or money by identifying each step in a business process and then revising or cutting out steps that do not create value (Bertagnolli 2018). The philosophy has its roots in Japan and operations, but is presently widely spread across the world and industries. Lean management focuses on:

- Putting the customer into the focus of operation
- Defining value and value-added from the standpoint of the end customer
- Eliminating all waste in all areas of the value chain

M. Helmold, *Lean Management and Kaizen*, Management for Professionals,
https://doi.org/10.1007/978-3-030-46981-8_1

- Continuously improving all activities, processes, purposes, and people
- Putting the people into the centre of value-adding services and processes

Lean management facilitates shared leadership and responsibility; continuous improvement ensures that every employee contributes to the improvement process. The management method acts as a guide to building a successful and solid organization that is constantly progressing, identifying real problems and resolving them.

Lean management is based on the Toyota production system which was established in the late 1940s. Toyota put into practice the five principles of lean management with the goal being to decrease the amount of processes that were not producing value; this became known as the Toyota Way. By implementing the five principles, they found that significant improvements were made in efficiency, productivity, cost-efficiency, and cycle time. Lean management incorporates five guiding principles that are used by managers within an organization as the guidelines to the lean methodology (Helmold and Samara 2019). The five principles are:

1. Identify value in all process of the value chain.
2. Conduct value stream mapping.
3. Create a continuous workflow.
4. Establish a pull system in which the customers are the focus.
5. Facilitate a continuous improvement culture.

Identifying value, the first step in lean management, means finding the problem that the customer needs solved and making the product the solution. Specifically, the product must be the part of the solution that the customer will readily pay for. Any process or activity that does not add value, meaning it does not add usefulness and the customer is not willing to pay for it, importance or worth to the final product is considered waste and should be eliminated (Liker 2004).

Value stream mapping refers to the process of mapping out the company's workflow, including all actions and people who contribute to the process of creating and delivering the end product to the consumer. Value stream mapping helps managers visualize which processes are led by what teams and identify the people responsible for measuring, evaluating, and improving the process. This visualization helps managers determine which parts of the system do not bring value to the workflow (Slack et al. 1995).

Creating a continuous workflow means ensuring each team's workflow progresses smoothly and preventing any interruptions or bottlenecks that may occur with cross-functional teamwork. Kanban, a lean management technique that utilizes a visual cue to trigger action, is used to enable easy communication between teams so they can address what needs to be done and when it needs to be done by. Breaking the total work process into a collection of smaller parts and visualizing the workflow in this regard facilitate the feasible removal of process interruptions and roadblocks.

Developing a pull system ensures that the continuous workflow remains stable and guarantees that the teams deliver work assignments faster and with less effort. A pull system is a specific lean technique that decreases the waste of any production process. It ensures that new work is only started if there is a demand for it, thus providing the advantage of minimizing overhead and optimizing storage costs.

The last principle is the continuous improvement and can be regarded as the most important step in the lean management method. Facilitating continuous improvement refers to a variety of techniques that are used to identify what an organization has done, what it needs to do, any possible obstacles that may arise and how all members of the organization can make their work processes better. The lean management system is neither isolated nor unchanging, and, therefore, issues may occur within any of the other four steps. Ensuring all employees contribute to the continuous improvement of the workflow protects the organization whenever problems emerge. Management has to create an environment and culture, in which all employees can work in line with the five principles (Ohno 1990; Bertagnolli 2018).

1.2 Lean Management Versus the Traditional Concept

In contrast to the traditional manufacturing concepts, the lean production is based on a reduction of throughput times, low inventories, and the permanent elimination of non-value-adding activities throughout the value chain (Ohno 1990). These (non-value-adding) activities are unnecessary and represent waste or "muda" (Japanese = 無駄).

Figure 1.1 shows the two concepts, the traditional and the lean one. Both concepts are directed towards customers. The lean management concept's foundation is based on the optimal reaction capability and not based on inventories. Inventories increase the cost of capital and have negative impacts on the shareholder value, whereas short cycle times lead to small inventories. Lean manufacturing or lean production, often simply "lean", is a systematic method for the elimination of waste ("muda") within a manufacturing system. Lean also takes into account waste created through overburden ("muri") and waste created through unevenness in workloads ("mura"). Working from the perspective of the client who consumes a product or service, "value" is any action or process that a customer would be willing to pay

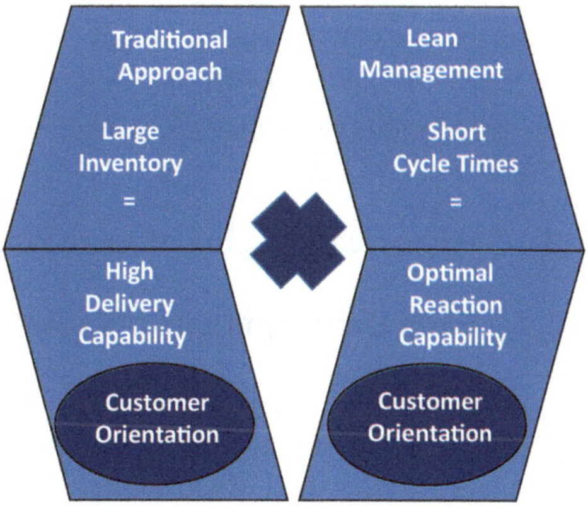

Fig. 1.1 Lean management versus traditional concept. (Source: Author's source)

for. Essentially, lean is centred on making obvious what adds value by reducing everything else. Lean manufacturing is a management philosophy derived mostly from the Toyota Production System (TPS) (hence the term Toyotism is also prevalent) and identified as "lean" only in the 1990s. TPS is renowned for its focus on reduction of the original Toyota seven wastes to improve overall customer value, but there are varying perspectives on how this is best achieved. The steady growth of Toyota, from a small company to the world's largest automaker, has focused attention on how it has achieved this success.

The key to acquiring and keeping customers is by offering value. To do this, we must first understand our customers and what they are willing to pay for – this is what we call "value". By definition, everything else is waste, diminishing value to the customer and reducing profitability. Put simply, lean thinking (or Toyota Way トヨタウエイ) is delivering value from the customer's perspective and eliminating waste (or muda 無駄). Lean is the combination of the five aforementioned complementary, interconnected principles, each geared towards increasing value to the customer by improving efficiency. By applying these simple principles, any business in any sector can not only provide a better service or product to their end users but also make fundamental, sustainable improvements in profitability. The Toyota Production System (TPS) has been adopted by many companies in all sectors on a global scale. The TPS has been applied by many OEMs in automotive industry, railway area, and other business sectors. Bombardier Transportation is applying the Bombardier Operations System (BOS), Porsche the Porsche Production System (PPS), and Daimler the Daimler Production System. However, it is not always successful, as the activities are only partially introduced and not rolled out in total. Secondly, lean principles are not synchronized with the supply side and may thus not show the desired effects and results. It does not make sense to establish only single lean instruments. It is of the utmost importance and a fundamental aspect of the lean concept that principles are applied in a total approach that involves the suppliers. In this respect, it is the crucial role of procurement and supplier relationship management to transfer this competency to its supply chain. Inefficiencies throughout the supply chain can thus be identified, waste can be eliminated, and processes can be harmonized in order to strive for continuous improvements. Continuous improvement (Japanese: kaizen) means small steps and is part of the lean philosophy. Data show that the complete transfer of lean principles to the own operation and the supply chain will lead to significant productivity improvements and significant cost reduction advantages of up to 15 to 50 percent (Liker 2004).

1.3 Historical Origins of Lean Management

1.3.1 Early Developments of Lean Management

Early developments of lean management tools reach back into the early times of industrialization. With increased customer demands, entrepreneurs were trying to implement processes that would accelerate and increase the production. Eli Whitney is most famous as the inventor of the cotton gin. However, the gin was a minor accomplishment compared to his perfection of interchangeable parts. Whitney developed this about 1799 when he took a contract from the US Army for the manufacture of 10,000 muskets at the unbelievably low price of $13.40 for each gun.

For the next 100 years, manufacturers primarily concerned themselves with individual technologies. During this time our system of engineering drawings developed, modern machine tools were perfected, and large-scale processes such as the Bessemer process for making steel held the centre of attention. As products moved from one discrete process to the next through the logistics system and within factories, few people concerned themselves with:

- What happens in between processes
- How multiple processes were arranged within the factory
- How the chain of processes functioned as a system
- How each worker went about a task

1.3.2 Ford and Taylorism

This changed in the late 1890s with the work of early industrial engineers. Frederick W. Taylor began to look at individual workers and work methods. The result was the studies of time management, the time per one cycle and standardized work operations. He called his ideas scientific management (Hounshell 1988). Taylor was a controversial manager and personality. The concept of applying science to management was sound, but Taylor simply ignored the behavioural sciences. In addition, he had a peculiar attitude towards factory workers. Frank Gilbreth (Cheaper by The Dozen) added motion study and invented process charting. Process charts focused attention on all work elements including those non-value-added elements which normally occur between the "official" elements. Lillian Gilbreth brought psychology into the mix by studying the motivations of workers and how attitudes affected the outcome of a process. There were, of course, many other contributors. These were the people who originated the idea of "eliminating waste", a key tenet of JIT and lean manufacturing. Although there are instances of rigorous process thinking in manufacturing all the way back to the Arsenal in Venice in the 1450s, the first person to truly integrate an entire production process was Henry Ford. At Highland Park, MI, in 1913, he married consistently interchangeable parts with standard work and moving conveyance to create what he called flow production. The public grasped this in the dramatic form of the moving assembly line, but from the standpoint of the manufacturing engineer, the breakthroughs actually went much further. Ford lined up fabrication steps in process sequence wherever possible using special-purpose machines and go/no-go gauges to fabricate and assemble the components going into the vehicle within a few minutes and deliver perfectly fitting components directly to lineside. This was a truly revolutionary break from the shop practices of the American System that consisted of general-purpose machines grouped by process, which made parts that eventually found their way into finished products after a good bit of tinkering (fitting) in subassembly and final assembly. The problem with Ford's system was not the flow: he was able to turn the inventories of the entire company every few days. Rather it was his inability to provide variety. The Model T was not just limited to one colour, which was black. It was also limited to one specification so that all Model T chassis were essentially identical up through the end of production in 1926. (The customer did have a choice of four or five body styles, a drop-on feature from outside suppliers added at the very end of the production line.) Indeed, it appears that practically every machine in the Ford Motor Company worked on a single part number, and there were essentially no changeovers. When the world wanted variety, including model cycles shorter than the 19 years for the Model T, Ford seemed to lose his way. Other automakers responded to the need for many models, each with many options, but with production systems whose design and fabrication steps regressed towards process areas with much longer throughput times. Over time they populated their fabrication shops with larger and larger machines that ran faster and faster, apparently lowering costs per process step, but continually increasing throughput times and inventories except in the rare case (like engine machining lines) where all of the process steps could be linked and automated (Hounshell 1988). Even worse, the time lags between process steps and the complex part routings required ever more sophisticated information management systems culminating in computerized materials requirements planning (MRP) systems.

1.3.3 Toyota Production System (TPS)

As Kiichiro Toyoda, Taiichi Ohno, and others at Toyota looked at this situation in the 1930s, and more intensely just after World War II, it occurred to them that a series of simple innovations might make it more possible to provide both continuity in process flow and a wide variety in product offerings. They therefore revisited Ford's original thinking and invented the Toyota Production System.

Fig. 1.2 Lean management and kaizen. (Source: Author's source)

This system in essence shifted the focus of the manufacturing engineer from individual machines and their utilization to the flow of the product through the total process. Toyota concluded that by right-sizing machines for the actual volume needed, introducing self-monitoring machines to ensure quality, lining the machines up in process sequence, pioneering quick setups so each machine could make small volumes of many part numbers, and having each process step notify the previous step of its current needs for materials, it would be possible to obtain low cost, high variety, high quality, and very rapid throughput times to respond to changing customer desires. The concept of the TPS is based on a paradigm of permanent and continuous improvement, the kaizen philosophy. Figure 1.2 displays the meaning of kaizen as change for the best or change for improvement. Also, information management could be made much simpler and more accurate (Liker 2004). The thought process of lean was thoroughly described in the book *The Machine That Changed the World* (1990) by Womack, Jones, and Roos; the authors described that lean principles are based on five elements:

1. Specify the value desired by the customer.
2. Identify the value stream for each product providing that value and challenge all of the wasted steps (generally nine out of ten) currently necessary to provide it.
3. Make the product flow continuously through the remaining value-added steps.
4. Introduce pull between all steps where continuous flow is possible.
5. Manage towards perfection so that the number of steps and the amount of time and information needed to serve the customer continually fall.

1.3.4 Lean Management in Today's World

This continued success has over the past two decades created an enormous demand for greater knowledge about lean thinking. There are literally hundreds of books and papers, not to mention thousands of media articles exploring the subject, and numerous other resources available to this growing audience. As lean thinking continues to spread to every country in the world, leaders are also adapting the tools and principles beyond manufacturing to logistics and distribution, services, retail, healthcare, construction, maintenance, and even government. Indeed, lean consciousness and methods are only beginning to take root among senior managers and leaders in all sectors today. Value chain networks in the present times are complex and international structures of supply and demand (Helmold and Terry 2016). Especially, Japanese makers show how suppliers are sustainably integrated into the own value chain and activities (James et al. 1997; Helmold and Terry 2016). The Japanese networks are described as "keiretsu networks", in which suppliers and customers are integrated systems throughout the value chain (Helmold and Samara 2019). Future lean management concepts and supply chains will be configured in a transparent and optimal way, so that wasteful activities and processes can be eliminated at the earliest point of time (Srai and Gregory 2008). In the future competitiveness will be decided on who has the most flexible and efficient value network including

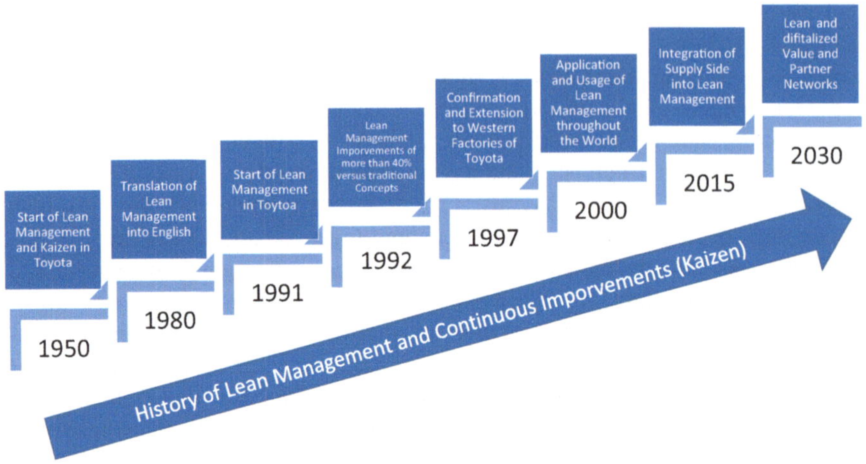

Fig. 1.3 Time line and development of lean management. (Source: Author's source)

value streams from raw material suppliers over the own operations to the distribution to the customers (Helmold and Terry 2016) (Fig. 1.3).

1.4 Lean Management in Japan

1.4.1 Lean Thinking as Part of the Japanese Culture

One of the biggest parts of this involves the concept of "kata". These are general societal rules and patterns of behaviours that the Japanese exhibit in their everyday life. Since this is an ingrained part of the Japanese culture, the standard practices of business come very naturally to people in this country. As part of their culture, the Japanese are also known for being perfectionists in everything that they do. They take a great deal of pride in their work, so they take a great deal of care to train their employees to ensure the highest quality of work. Another big part of this concept of lean is listening and patience. Toyota is a company that has been heavily associated with lean. One of the things that makes this company so unique is that rather than just barking orders, they encourage workers to develop their own skills and problem-solving abilities. There is also a focus more on the long-term goals of a company rather than the short-term. These are all areas that exemplify how crucial patience is to the Japanese culture. In fact, to be considered an expert in any field, it takes a great deal of time, so patience is necessary. Lean is all about how you organize a business to make it more efficient. The purpose is to maximize value and reduce waste. The Japanese culture is known for valuing cleanliness and order, both in the way they live their everyday life and how they run their businesses. If everything is meticulously organized, you can reduce waste because you know exactly what you have and what you need. This applies to office supplies and workflow management.

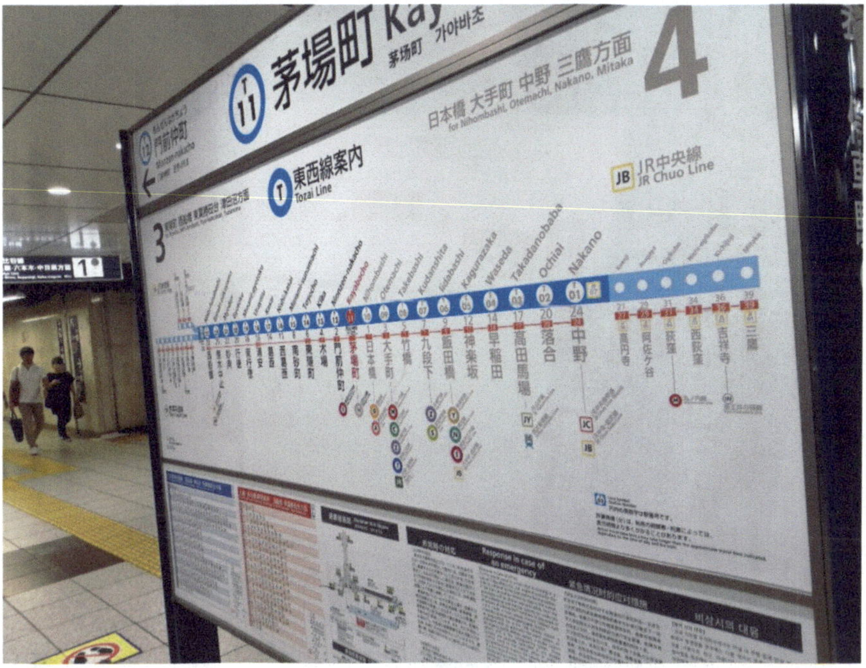

Fig. 1.4 Visualization in Tokyo Metro. (Source: Author's source)

You are able to see who should be working on what to know what needs to get done. It makes the business run more efficiently. Figure 1.4 shows how lean tools of visualization are integrated inside the Japanese society and life. It shows the Tozai Line including information on connections, time, and also the location. Other lines and connections are marked in different colours. Another example of lean management and artificial intelligence is a bakery in Tokyo (Fig. 1.5), where the customer-selected products are identified through a camera on a special counter. The staff only needs to confirm, so that the price is shown to the customer. The customer can now pay via telephone payment (one scan), via card, or via inserting money into a slot. The change is given automatically. The process is very fast, waste like waiting time is eliminated, and the staff can use more time to advise and assist customers.

1.4.2 Influences of Bushido: Seven Virtues

Bushido is the definition for the code of ethics and ideals that dictated the samurai way of life in ancient Japan. The moral values of samurai warriors are stressing elements like sincerity, frugality, loyalty, martial arts, and honour until death. Bushido flourished during the Edo period from 1600 to 1878. Inspired from neo-Confucianism during the Edo period and influenced by Shinto and Buddhism, it allowed the

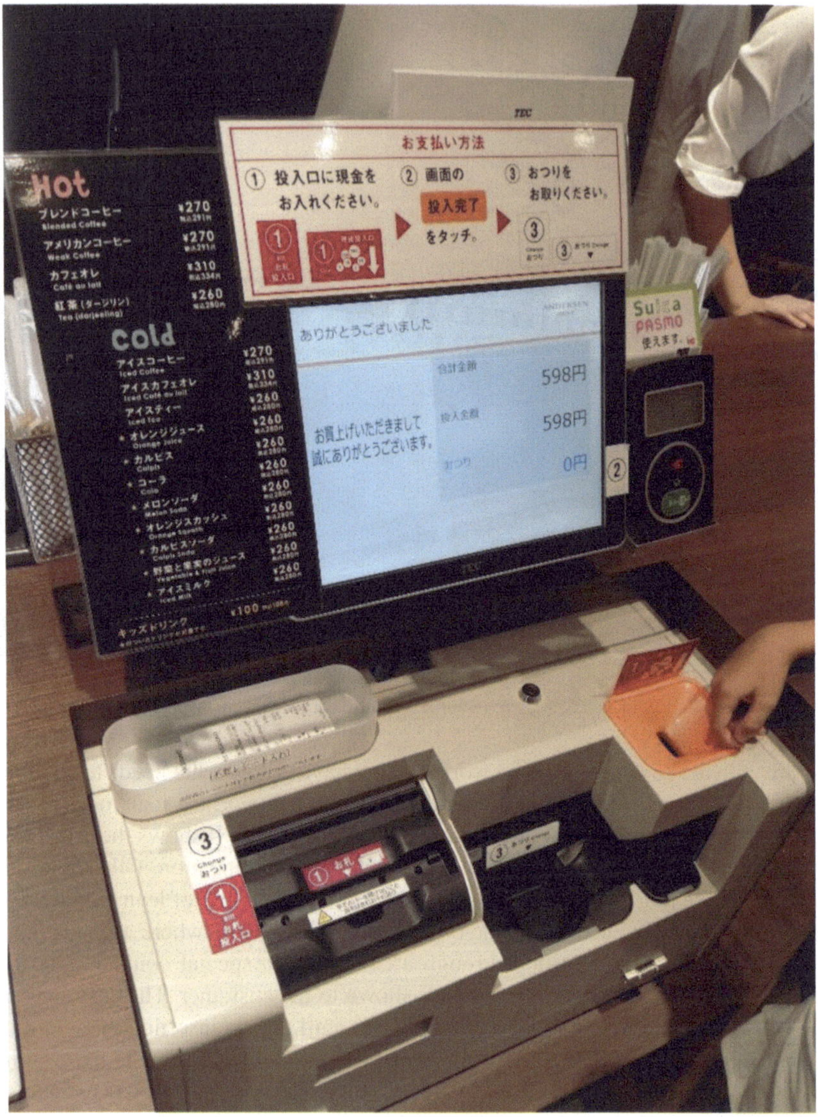

Fig. 1.5 Artificial intelligence in a bakery in Tokyo. (Source: Author's source)

samurai to be tempered by wisdom, patience, and serenity. The seven virtues are shown in Fig. 1.6 and are defined as follows:

1. Justice or Rectitude (義 gi)

   This is all about making sure that we have the right way when we make a decision and that we have the power to make a decision quickly. It is about

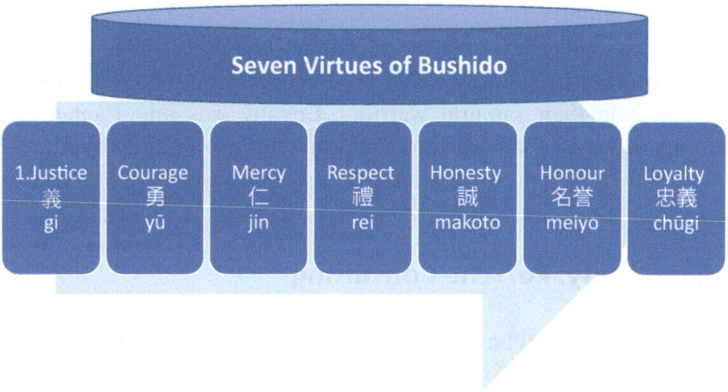

Fig. 1.6 Seven virtues of bushido. (Source: Author's source)

making sure that we do not become indecisive and that our decisions are made and based on the right reasons.

2. Courage (勇 yū)

   This is about making sure that what we do is right and that we have the courage to do the right thing and not just what people think we should do. If we are raised in a particular way, we think in a way that we believe in. This is about making sure we do what we believe in and have the courage to do so.

3. Benevolence or Mercy (仁 jin)

   As a warrior, the samurai have the power to kill. However, benevolence is about making sure that you are balanced in how you think. It is about making sure that you also have sympathy and mercy at the right time. For the samurai it was about making sure you fought for the right reason and that if you had to kill someone, you did it for the right reason and your belief but that you also make sure that if there was no need to kill, you would have mercy and be sympathetic.

4. Respect (禮 rei)

   It is important that in everything they believe, they must have respect and be polite in everything. The way they live their life meant they must be respectful of their elders, they must respect life, and respect others beliefs.

5. Honesty (誠 makoto)

   Honesty was very important, as they believe that being honest in everything you do gives you respect and means you can be trusted.

6. Honour (名誉 meiyo)

   To live and die with honour was very important to the samurai. Everything they did was honourable which meant they did everything in what they believed with honour.

7. Loyalty (忠義 chūgi)

   Loyalty was probably one of the very important parts of what they did. They treated each other like family and would do everything within their power to protect and help their samurai warriors. Loyalty was important because this means they can trust their warriors and know they would be loyal to whatever they needed to do and not worry about losing their respect.

1.5 Case Study: Porsche Consulting

Practical examples by Porsche Consulting show that the introduction of the TPS led to radical improvements in terms of errors and defects per car (quality), serial completion time (cost and productivity), and inventory (logistics and delivery). The study reveals that the reduction of defects per car was reduced by 63 percent. The throughput time could be improved by more than 53 percent. This caused a positive situation of inventory by 50 percent. In the JIT approach, it is important that the right part comes in the right quantity in the right quality at the right time to the right place as shown in the 7R principle. This principle focuses on a zero defect as shown in the next figure. This principle was defined in the previous chapters as part of the objectives. The principles can be regarded as obtaining the right parts at the right quality and at the right time. This has to be in line with the right quantity in the right place by the right people at the right price (Helmold and Samara 2019). Companies such as Porsche have understood that the low value-adding activities of the own organization lead automatically to increasing activities on the supply side (Kalkowsky 2004). Porsche was also hampered by antiquated production methods. Some 20 percent of its parts were delivered 3 or more days too late, for example. The former head of Porsche, Dr. Wendelin Wiedeking, who had been deeply impressed by what he had seen on visits to Japanese auto firms such as Toyota, Nissan, and Honda, believed that only a radical, "lean manufacturing" cure would save the company. He flew in teams of the same Japanese consultants who had helped Toyota and gave them free rein. "A cultural revolution from top to bottom" is the way he describes what happened next, as the consultants organized the workforce into teams and one by one eliminated poor practices. Wiedeking made one now-fabled appearance on the assembly line wielding a circular saw, which he used to cut down the roof-high racks of spare parts that towered over the production line. After the lean cure of the own production facilities, Porsche extended the lean concept to suppliers and established the supplier development department in 2006 (the name of the department is FEL, Finance-Purchasing, Supply Management). This department is in charge of extending lean principles to the supply networks and to synchronize production systems. In the following section, the concept of lean supply management will be discussed. Lean principles have:

- To apply lean principles throughout the supply chain
- To integrate suppliers

Fig. 1.7 Lean management and kaizen (Source. Author's source)

- To be customer oriented
- To have a flat and transparent hierarchy
- To establish competencies to core functions
- To apply lean principles to shop floor (gemba)
- To concentrate only on essential success factors
- To reduce waste
- To continuously improve
- To apply a pull system
- To apply a learning organization

Figure 1.7 shows the Porsche production assembly including a one-piece flow. Porsche is implementing the principles of a just-in-time production system.

References

Bertagnolli, F. (2018). *Lean Management*. Wiesbaden: Springer.

James, R., Lincoln, M. L., Takahashi, G., & Takahashi, P. (1997). Keiretsu networks in the Japanese economy: An analysis of Intercorporate ties. *American Sociological Review., 57*(5), 561–585.

Helmold, M., & Terry, B. (2016). *Global sourcing and supply management excellence in China. Procurement guide for supply experts*. Singapore: Springer.

Helmold, M., & Samara, W. (2019). *Progress in performance management. Industry insights and case studies on principles, application tools, and practice*. Heidelberg: Springer.

Hounshell, David A. (1988). Organisational Structure. The same old principles in the New Manufacturing. Harvard Business Review. Retrieved 25 Nov 2019. https://hbr.org/1988/11/the-same-old-principles-in-the-new-manufacturing.

Kalkowsky, M. (2004). Nur Porsche hat das lean management begriffen: Interview with prof. D. Jones. *PRO, 31*, 16.

Liker, J. K. (2004). *The Toyota way*. Madison: McGraw-Hill.

Ohno, T. (1990). *Toyota production system. Beyond large scale production*. New York: Productivity Press.

Slack, N., et al. (1995). *Operations management*. London: Pitman Publishing.

Srai, J. S., & Gregory, M. F. (2008). A supply network configuration perspective on international supply chain development. *International Journal of Operations & Production Management., 28*(5), 386–411.

2 The Cultural Change Towards Lean Management

Perfection is not attainable. But if we chase perfection, we can catch excellence.

Vince Lombardi (1913–1970)

2.1 Lean Management as Part of the Organizational Culture

Lean management and processes have positive effects on the performance of the organization in terms of quality cost, delivery, and other improvements. However, it is necessary to establish organizational infrastructures which required for effective lean implementation and continuation (Fatma 2015). The Cultural Web, developed by Gerry Johnson and Kevan Scholes in 1992, provides one such approach for looking at and changing your organization's culture. Using it, you can expose cultural assumptions and practices and set to work aligning organizational elements with one another and with your strategy. These infrastructures must integrate cultural elements as illustrated in Fig. 2.1. The challenge to implement and sustain lean management processes lies in the need to identify the organizational culture infrastructure that will allow this system that was first used by Japanese firms to operate well in other organizational contexts. The values and norms that underlie lean processes may create conflict with the culture that already exists within the organization; such divergence retards adoption and performance (Helmold and Samara 2019). Johnson and Scholes identified six distinct but interrelated elements which contribute to what they called the "paradigm", equivalent to the pattern of the work environment, or the values of the organization. They suggested that each may be examined and analysed individually to gain a clearer picture of the wider cultural issues of an organization. The six contributing elements (with example questions used to examine the organization at hand) are as follows.

M. Helmold, *Lean Management and Kaizen*, Management for Professionals,
https://doi.org/10.1007/978-3-030-46981-8_2

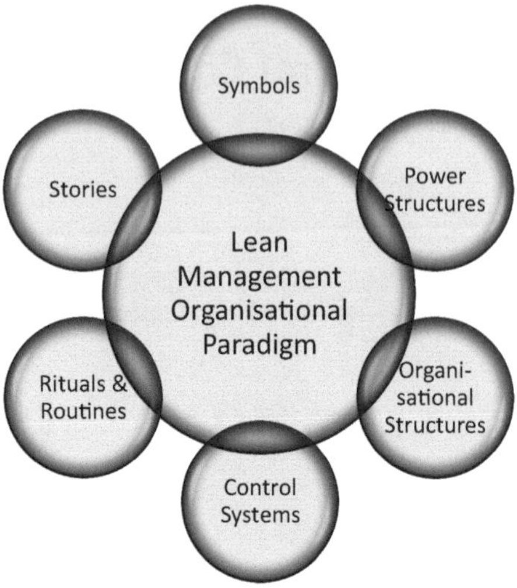

Fig. 2.1 Lean management cultural paradigm. (Source: Author's source, adopted from Johnson and Scholes 1997)

2.1.1 Stories and Myths

These are the previous events and happenings, both accurate and not, which are discussed by individuals within and outside the enterprise. This element deals with the questions and which events and people are remembered by the company or not. It indicates what the company values and what it chooses to immortalize through stories. Questions concerning the stories and myths are:

- What form of company reputation is communicated between customers and stakeholders?
- What stories do people tell new employees about the company?
- What do people know about the history of the organization?
- What do these stories say about the culture of the business?

2.1.2 Rituals and Routines

The rituals and routines category refers to the daily actions and behaviours of individuals within the organization. Routines indicate what is expected of employees on a day-to-day basis and what has been either directly or indirectly approved by those in managerial positions. Questions in this category are:

- What do employees expect when they arrive each day?
- What experience do customers expect from the organization?
- What would be obvious if it were removed from routines?
- What do these rituals and routines say about organizational beliefs?

2.1.3 Symbols

This element, symbols, deals with the visual representation of the company: how they appear to both employees and individuals on the outside. It includes logos, office spaces, dress codes, and sometimes advertisements. Questions are:

- What kind of image is associated with the company from the outside?
- How do employees and managers view the organization?
- Are there any company-specific designs or jargon used?
- How does the organization advertise itself?

2.1.4 Control Systems

Control systems are the systems and pathways by which the organization is controlled. This can refer to many things, including financial management, individual performance-based rewards (both measurement and distribution), and quality-control structures. Questions that must be tackled in this respect are:

- Which processes are strongly and weakly controlled?
- In general, is the company loosely or tightly controlled?
- Are employees rewarded or punished for performance?
- What reports and processes are used to keep control of finance, etc.?

2.1.5 Organizational Structures

This aspect refers to both the hierarchy and structure designated by the organization. Alongside this, Johnson and Scholes also use it to refer to the unwritten power and influence that some members may exert, which also indicate whose contributions to the organization are most valued by those above them.

- How hierarchical is the organization?
- Is responsibility and influence distributed in a formal or informal way?
- Where are the official lines of authority?
- Are there any unofficial lines of authority?

2.1.6 Power Structures

This element is referring to the genuine power structures and responsible individuals within the organization. It may refer to a few executives, the CEO, board members, or an entire managerial division. These individuals are those who hold the greatest influence over decisions and generally have the final say on major actions or changes.

- Who holds the power within the organization?
- Who makes decisions on behalf of the company?
- What are the beliefs and culture of those as the top of the business?
- How is power used within the organization?

2.1.7 Cultural Web to Change

As above, the first step of changing the culture of the organization is to analyse elements of the Cultural Web as they are in the present. The next step is to repeat the process, examining each element, but this time considering what one would like the culture, beliefs, and systems to be. This can then subsequently be compared with the ideal culture, and the differences between the two can be used to develop achievable steps towards change within the company. One will likely only then realize the true strengths and weaknesses of the organization's current culture, what the various hindrances are to growth, and how to go about changing specific elements to develop and achieve success. A new strategy can evolve from this by looking at introducing new beliefs and prioritizing positive reinforcement of current, successful ones. Hopefully, by integrating this system of analysis, managers can find themselves able to break free of ritual and belief systems within a company to achieve real change and innovation.

2.2 Need for Change of Organizational Culture

Successful organizations do not prosper by devoting a ruthless approach to chip away at costs, relentlessly reducing all decision-making to a reduction in head count. The purpose of lean culture change is to secure the future of the entity by uniting its people to deliver to the voice of the customer. In the not for profit sector, lean culture change drives organizational success by adding value to existing consumers and winning loyalty. It is about developing resilient service provision, developing core staff competencies and attracting and retaining the best people. The lean culture reverses the polarity of the organization shifting from a fire-fighting mode to a planning mode, where prevention of problems rather than reacting after the event of failure becomes the norm. Healthy, positive, organizational cultures are characterized by a long-term continuity perspective, with a focus on tactics to resolve immediate short-term problems. The dominant culture should support and reward cross-organizational working. Implementing lean thinking is a cultural change that requires leadership because in the end it's all about people. Here are ten guidelines your leader can do right now to change the culture.

Challenge People to Think

If you are not thinking, you're not learning new things. If you're not learning, you're not growing – and over time becoming irrelevant in your work. The most successful leaders understand their colleagues' mindsets, capabilities, and areas for improvement. They use this knowledge/insight to challenge their teams to think and stretch them to reach for more.

Lead by Example

Leading by example sounds easy, but few leaders are consistent with this one. Successful leaders practice what they preach and are mindful of their actions. They know everyone is watching them and therefore are incredibly intuitive about detecting those who are observing their every move, waiting to detect a performance shortfall.

Take Lots of Leaps of Faith

Making a change requires a leap of faith. Taking that leap of faith is risky, and people will only take active steps towards the unknown if they genuinely believe – and perhaps more importantly feel – that the risks of standing still are greater than those of moving forward in a new direction. Making a change takes lots of leaps of faith.

Create an Environment Where It Is Okay to Fail

Failure should be encouraged! That's right. If you don't try, you can't grow; and if growth is what you seek, failing is inevitable. There must be encouragement to try and it's okay if you try and it doesn't work. An environment where you can't fail creates fear.

Eliminate Concrete Heads

"Concrete heads" is the Japanese term for someone who does not accept that the organization must be focused on the elimination of waste. People feel threatened by the changes brought about by lean. As waste and bureaucracy are eliminated, some will find that little of what they have been doing is adding value. The anxiety they feel is normal and expected. To counteract this, it is critical that people are shown how the concept of work needs to change.

Be a Great Teacher

Successful leaders take the time to mentor their colleagues and make the investment to sponsor those who have proven they are able and eager to advance. They never stop teaching because they are so self-motivated to learn themselves.

Show Respect to Everyone

Everyone desires respect. Everyone. Regardless of your position or power, ensure you show everyone respect. Everyone wants to be treated fairly.

Motivate Your Followers

Transformational leaders provide inspirational motivation to encourage their followers to get into action. Of course, being inspirational isn't always easy. Some ideas for leadership inspiration include being genuinely passionate about ideas or goals, helping followers feel included in the process, and offering recognition, praise, and rewards for people's accomplishments.

Develop a True Team Environment
Create an environment where working as a team is valued and encouraged and where individuals work together to solve problems and help move the organization forward. Individuals who will challenge each other and support each other make teams more successful.

Encourage People to Make Contributions
Let the members of your team know that you welcome their ideas. Leaders who encourage involvement from group members has shown to lead to greater commitment, more creative problem-solving, and improved productivity.

Constant change is a business reality, and organizations must continually adapt to their environments to stay competitive or risk losing relevance and becoming obsolete. For each change, leaders must define it, create a vision of the post-change world, and mobilize their teams to make it.

Fundamentally, a change of culture occurs when people start behaving differently as a result of a change in the climate of the organization. There are many different models of how an organizational culture is shaped by the prevailing climate and how it can be assessed. Leaders who protect the status quo through control must surrender to change in order to secure the future for their organization. Don't be the leader who rewards herd mentality and me too thinking. Don't be the leader who encourages people not to fail or not to take risks. Be the leader who both models and gives permission to do the exact opposite of the aforementioned – be a leader who leads. The culture of an organization is learnt over time. It can be taught to new employees through formal training programs but is more generally absorbed through stories, myths, rituals, and shared behaviours within teams. Organizational culture will impact positively or negatively on everything you try to do whether you want it to or not.

2.3 Creating a Logical and Open Mind

Chiiku (知育) means to master intellectual knowledge and develop logical thinking for fundamental survival skills. For businesses to stay profitable, they first need stability based on a concrete understanding of their needs and priorities. Then, by using their uncovered resources, they can begin to innovate. Understanding this fundamental need for the business's survival is the foundation of future prosperity, and it should also form the foundation for developing leaders within the workplace. Chiiku focuses on this logical understanding of the business in a larger context. This is like envisioning a forest as an entire ecosystem rather than just a collection of trees. For business leaders, chiiku means to calculate the sense of urgency and communicate it at all times.

2.4 Leadership Development and Culture

Tokuiku(徳育) kuiku means to develop your rational interpersonal skills as a leader. Rational development (tokuiku) is different from logical development (chiiku). Logical thinking is based on cause and effect, whereas rational thinking is based on quantity and scale. Logical thinking can tell us what we ought to do, but we need to be rational to understand why it benefits each individual. It is necessary for humans to develop themselves by not staying satisfied with the current state and rationally comparing it to other possibilities. Leaders must first develop the courage to take risks and surpass the status quo. This is like ensuring the survival of the forest by understanding the needs of each organism that makes up the ecosystem. While chiiku is focused on the organization's survival as an entity, tokuiku focuses on ensuring the enrichment and success of the individuals who make up that entity.

2.5 Emotional and Physical Strength

Taiiku (体育): Modern education systems understand taiiku as physical education (PE). It is seen as simply a way to make students exercise their bodies through sports. But physical education is about more than just building muscles and developing a sense of competitiveness. Taiiku first focuses on strengthening one's willpower and emotions to force out the right actions. For business leaders, taiiku means learning the skills to inspire a culture of immediate action, not just the words. Leaders must learn to help others break the status quo. This means learning the self-criticism mentality (hansei).

2.6 Case Study: Toyota

Toyota Motor Corporation's organizational culture defines the responses of employees to challenges the company faces in the market. As a global leader in the automobile industry, Toyota uses its organizational culture to maximize human resource capabilities in innovation. The company also benefits from its organizational culture in terms of support for problem-solving. The different features or characteristics of Toyota's organizational culture indicate a careful approach in facilitating organizational learning. The firm undergoes considerable change once in a while, as reflected in the change in its organizational structure in 2013. Toyota's organizational culture highlights the importance of developing an appropriate culture to support global business success. Toyota's organizational culture effectively supports the company's endeavours in innovation and continuous improvement. An understanding of this corporate culture is beneficial for identifying beliefs and principles that contribute to the strength of the firm's business and brands. Following its reorganization implemented in 2013, Toyota's organizational culture underwent corresponding change. Prior to 2013, its organizational culture emphasized a sense of hierarchy and secrecy, which translated to employees' perception that all decisions must come from the headquarters in Japan. However, after 2013, the characteristics of Toyota's organizational culture are as follows, arranged according to significance:

- Teamwork
- Continuous improvement through learning
- Quality
- Secrecy

Teamwork

Toyota uses teams in most of its business areas. One of the company's principles is that the synergy of teamwork leads to greater capabilities and success. This part of the organizational culture emphasizes the involvement of employees in their respective teams. To ensure that teamwork is properly integrated in the organizational culture, every Toyota employee goes through a team-building training program (Toyota, 2015a, b). Toyota's organizational culture facilitates the development of the firm as a learning organization. A learning organization utilizes information gained through the activities of individual workers to develop policies and programs for better results. Toyota's organizational culture highlights learning as a way of developing solutions to problems. In this way, the company is able to continuously improve processes and output with the support of its organizational culture. Quality is at the heart of Toyota's organizational culture. The success of the company is typically attributed to its ability to provide high-quality automobiles. To effectively integrate quality in its organizational culture, the firm uses Principle #5 of The Toyota Way, which says, "build a culture of stopping to fix problems, to get quality right the first time". The Toyota Way is a set of principles that defines the business approaches used in Toyota's organizational culture that has a considerable degree of secrecy. However, the level of secrecy has declined in recent years following the reorganization of the company in 2013. Before 2013, information about problems encountered in the workplace must go through the firm's headquarters in Toyota City, Japan. However, following the reorganization, the company's organizational culture now does not emphasize secrecy as much. For example, problems encountered in US plants are now disseminated, analysed, and solved within the North American business unit of Toyota. The characteristics of Toyota's organizational culture enable the company to continue growing. Innovation is based on continuous improvement through learning. Quality improvement and problem-solving are achieved through the activities of work teams. However, the secrecy feature of Toyota's organizational culture presents possible drawbacks because it reduces organizational flexibility in rapid problem-solving (Toyota, 2015a, b). Figure 2.2 shows a lean workshop conducted by the General Manager and his lean team experts, Dr. Marc Helmold, in China.

Fig. 2.2 Group of Bombardier in China. (Source: Author's source)

References

Fatma, P. (2015). The effect of organizational culture on implementing and sustaining lean processes. *Journal of Manufacturing Technology Management, 26*(5), 725–743.

Johnson, G., & Scholes, K. (1997). Exploring Corporate Strategy. Text and Cases. 4th Edition. Prentice Hall London.

Helmold, M., & Samara, W. (2019). *Progress in performance management. Industry insights and case studies on principles, application tools, and practice. Management for Professionals.* Heidelberg: Springer.

Toyota Motor Corporation (2015a). Guiding principles at Toyota.

Toyota Motor Corporation (2015b). Toyota way 2001.

Kaizen: Continuous Improvements in Small Steps

3

Logic will get you from A to B. Imagination will take you everywhere.

Albert Einstein (1879–1955)

3.1 Definition of Kaizen

Kaizen is a Japanese management concept and targets improvements in small steps. Kaizen means all personnel are expected to stop their work when they encounter any abnormality and, along with their supervisor, suggest an improvement to resolve the abnormality. Kaizen has the aim to be applied in daily life and routines, not only during working hours. The improvement should be gradual and infinite. It should pursue the perfection. The employees should be continuously engaged in company's life and improvement of every aspect of the company (processes, products, infrastructure, etc.). This improvement throughout all aspects of life is related to the great attention that is paid to needs and requirements of customer (Helmold et al. 2017).

Kaizen focuses on teams (quality circles) and promotes teamwork and team spirit; however, it also recognizes the individual contribution. It emphasizes the engagement of each worker to the concept and vision of the company, so that employees will identify themselves with the enterprise and its culture and objectives (Helmold and Samara 2019). The important aspects of kaizen are:

- What is wrong? Not who is wrong?
- How to eliminate waste (muda)?
- How to decrease quality costs?

M. Helmold, *Lean Management and Kaizen*, Management for Professionals, https://doi.org/10.1007/978-3-030-46981-8_3

The term kaizen is Japanese and can be translated to "change for the better". The main goal of kaizen is to continuously improve working areas, processes, and products by integrating the people of the affected areas. Usually kaizen is realized through workshops. Their typical duration can vary from 3 to 5 days. The aim of a kaizen workshop is to implement the improvements during the time of the workshop or shortly afterwards; kaizen is a framework combining the change of the company culture together with the daily implementation of the principles (Liker 2004). The ten principles of kaizen can be described as follows:

1. Say no to status quo.
2. If something is wrong, correct it.
3. Accept no excuses and make things happen.
4. Improve everything continuously.
5. Abolish old, traditional concepts.
6. Be economical.
7. Empower everyone to take part in problem-solving.
8. Before making decisions, ask "why" five times to get to the root cause.
9. Get information and opinions from multiple people.
10. Remember that improvement has no limit; never stop trying to improve.

A useful tool in the context of kaizen is the PDCA cycle. PDCA is an iterative four-step management method used in business for the control and continuous improvement of processes and products. It is also known as the Deming circle/cycle/wheel and the Shewhart cycle. The PDCA cycle is since the 1950s recognized as a simplified illustration of the elementary steps of a continuous improvement process:

Plan: Analyse the current situation and define improvement plan.
Do: Implement the defined solutions.
Check: Evaluation of improvement results.
Act: Definition of counteractions in case of deviation from objective, standardize the best solution.

After improvement it is important to standardize and implement the action, so that the process or activity cannot return to the old state. If this is secured, one can aim for the next improvement.

3.2 Kaizen Versus Innovation

Kaizen (改善) is the concept of small improvements in small steps as shown in Fig. 3.1 (Ohno 1990). In contrast to an innovation, which is a top-down approach, kaizen involves all team members. It means improvement and continuing improvement in personal life, home life, social life, and working life. When applied to the workplace, this philosophy means continuing improvement involving everyone, i.e. managers and workers alike (Kaizen institute 2019). The principles are of kaizen are

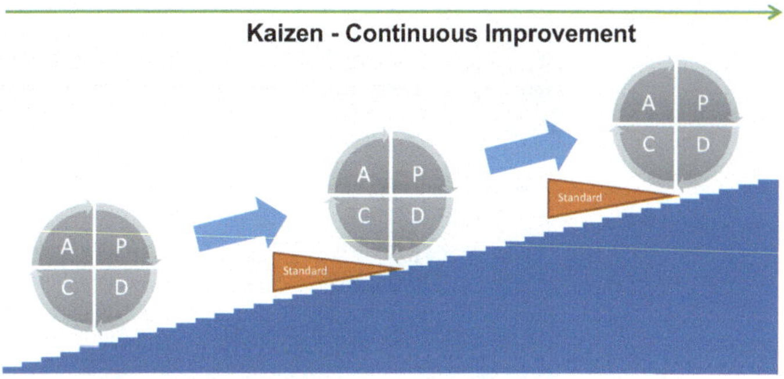

Fig. 3.1 Kaizen cycle (PDCA). (Source: Author's source)

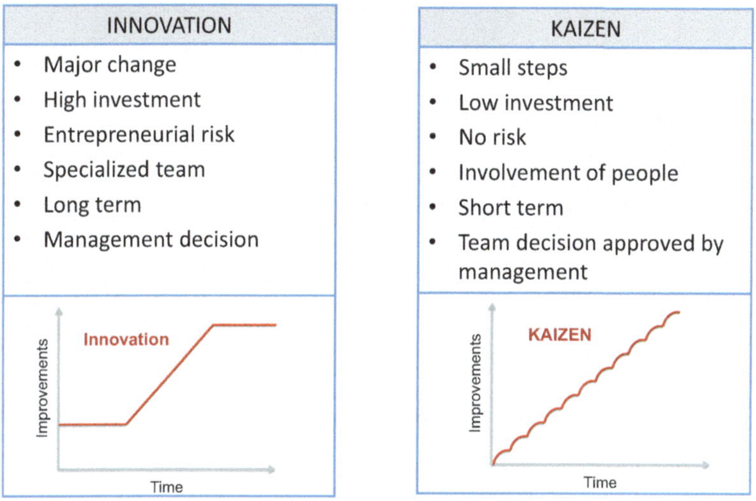

Fig. 3.2 Innovation versus kaizen. (Source: Author's source)

customer knowledge and transparency. Thus, it is possible to improve a process without major investments. Kaizen in any organization is fundamentally important for a successful continuous improvement culture and to mark a turning point in the progression of quality, productivity, and labour-management relations (Kaizen Institute 2019) (Fig. 3.2).

3.3 Visualization Management

Visualization management is a significant part of kaizen. Figure 3.1 displays that 83 percent of the issues are perceived with the eye sense, so that visualization is a crucial part for implementing kaizen (Fig. 3.3). Figure 3.4 shows the war room in the Bombardier Transportation IPO in China.

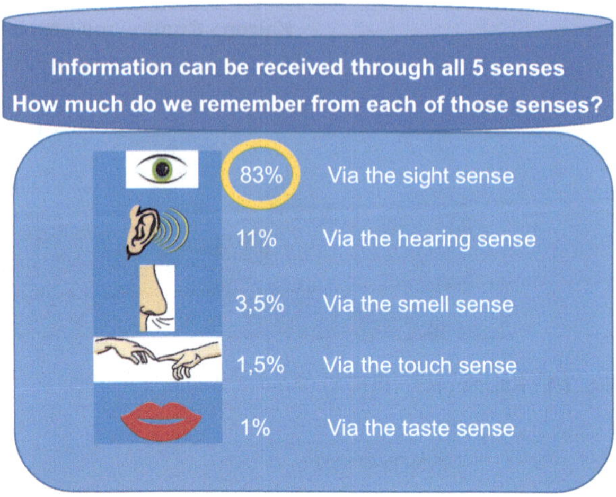

Fig. 3.3 Visualization senses. (Source: Author's source)

Fig. 3.4 Visualization examples. (Source: Author's source)

3.4 Case Study: Mercedes-Benz` Lean Management System

"The best or nothing" – Gottlieb Daimler's claim – characterizes the Mercedes-Benz brand and is anything but easy to live up to. What originally referred primarily to the ideas and ingenuity of the company's founder has since become more pragmatic (Follmann et al. 2013). Daimler is now a global organization with over 260,000 staff members and requires a clear vision, experienced and competent managers and employees, stable processes, and a strong corporate culture. The success of the automotive company hinges on the efforts of each individual. One of the important success factors to this end is a far-reaching production system. Production systems have a long tradition and clear principles. Back in 1831, for example, General Carl von Clausewitz recognized the importance of robust processes, avoiding waste and ensuring continuous improvement as necessary to achieve goals. The best-known production system currently used is that of Toyota. The production system used by Mercedes-Benz Cars (MBC) also has a long tradition and has become one of the driving factors behind the success of the premium Mercedes Benz brand – with a pronounced focus on technology, innovation, quality, safety, and sustainability. In 2000, this system was bundled as a closed system for the first time – the Mercedes-Benz Production System (MPS) – by leveraging different developments in the company. This laid the foundation for lean management principles in production and, somewhat later on, in administration. From a critical perspective, initial success was confronted by the challenges of early lean initiatives. Improvements in the individual business units, for example, could not be made at the expense of other business units (e.g. the historical conflict of assembly processes being compromised in the name of logistics and vice versa, or assuming that active involvement of managers in optimization measures is all that is required to safeguard changes and prevent relapses from occurring). To meet these challenges and facilitate implementation of the MPS, all resources were bundled at MBC in 2008. The organization was restructured, and four new consulting fields were defined: strategic and tactical target definition, methods and tools, qualification, and Mercedes-Benz culture. Today, almost 4 years after the go-ahead, an initial conclusion can be drawn. The introduction of centralized MPS was done in 2008. The framework provides all employees a standardized basis for the decentralized lean support organization at Mercedes-Benz Cars and anchored it in the "Strategische Planung und Mercedes-Benz Produktionssystem" (Strategic Planning and Mercedes-Benz Production System) centre. This centre is, among others, responsible for assisting business units in implementing the MPS throughout Mercedes-Benz Cars. Activities started in the production area and have since carried over to administrative areas such as human resources and IT.

References

Follmann, J., Laack, S., Schütt, H., & Uhl, A. (2013). Lean transformation at Mercedes-Benz. Retrieved 24 Nov 2019. https://www.researchgate.net/publication/272484962_Lean_Transformation_at_Mercedes-Benz_Identifying_the_Transformational_Opportunities_for_the_Retail_Value_Chain

Helmold, M. & Dathe, T., & Büsch, M. (2017). Praxisbericht aus der Bahnindustrie – Bombardier Transportation. Veränderte Anforderungen durch Global Sourcing. In Beschaffung aktuell. 4.5.2017. Retrieved 17 May 2018. https://beschaffung-aktuell.industrie.de/einkauf/veraenderte-anforderungen-durch-global-sourcing/.

Helmold, M., & Samara, W. (2019). *Progress in performance management. Industry insights and case studies on principles, application tools, and practice. Management for professionals.* Heidelberg: Springer.

Kaizen Institute. (2019). https://de.kaizen.com/.

Liker, J. K. (2004). *The Toyota way*. Madison: McGraw-Hill.

Ohno, T. (1990). *Toyota production system. Beyond large scale production*. New York: Productivity Press.

4 Waste and Value-Added

Most Business Processes Are 90 percent Waste and 10 percent Value-Added Work.

Jeffrey Liker

4.1 Value-Adding Activities and Waste

Added value can be defined as products, services, processes, and activities, which generate a certain value to the organization and enterprise. Value-added must be regarded from the customer viewpoint and is everything for which the customer is willing to pay for. It is important that value-added is recognized and perceived as value by the client. Many studies have shown that we only add value to a product for less than 5–15 percent of the time; the rest of the time is wasted (Helmold and Terry 2016a, b). The opposite is non-adding value or waste as shown in Fig. 4.1. Waste (Japanese: muda, 無駄) is anything which adds cost or time without adding any value, or any activity which does not satisfy any of the above conditions of value-added is a waste or a non-value-adding activity in a process. The focus in operations management must therefore be in eliminating such activities like waiting time or rework (Ohno 1990; Liker 2004). Enterprise must target value-added process and eliminate or reduce waste, whereby waste can be visible (obvious) or invisible (hidden) as shown in Fig. 4.2.

4.2 Ishikawa Diagrams to Identify Waste

Ishikawa diagrams (also called fishbone diagrams, herringbone diagrams, cause-and-effect diagrams, or Fishikawa) are causal diagrams created by Kaoru Ishikawa (Japanese: 石川 馨 Ishikawa Kaoru, 1915–1989) that show the cause-effect

M. Helmold, *Lean Management and Kaizen*, Management for Professionals,
https://doi.org/10.1007/978-3-030-46981-8_4

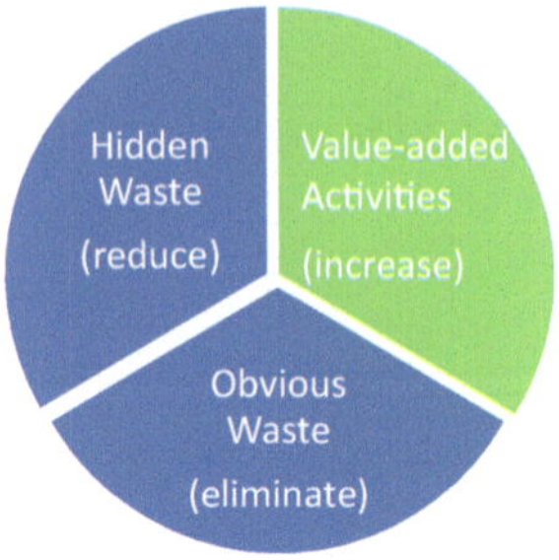

Fig. 4.1 Value-added and waste. (Source: Marc Helmold)

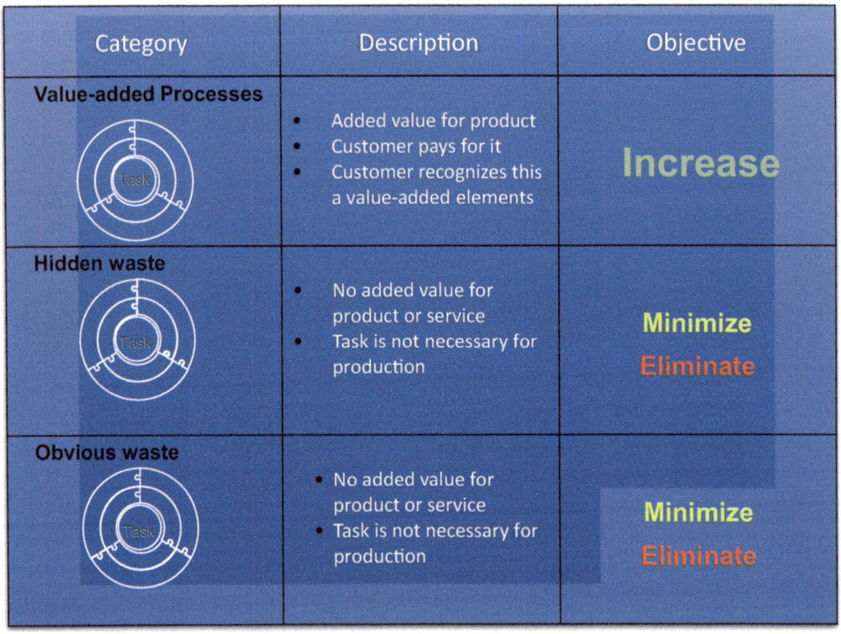

Fig. 4.2 Actions for value-added and waste. (Source: Marc Helmold)

situation of a specific event. Common uses of the Ishikawa diagram are areas of design, supply, production, and quality defect prevention to identify potential factors causing an overall effect. Each cause or reason for imperfection is a source of variation. Causes are usually grouped into major categories to identify and classify these sources of variation. The target of value-added and quality is shown as the fish's head, facing to the right, with the causes extending to the left as fishbones; the ribs branch off the backbone for major causes, with sub-branches for root causes, to as many levels as required. Figures 4.3 and 4.4 show two examples of the Ishikawa diagram.

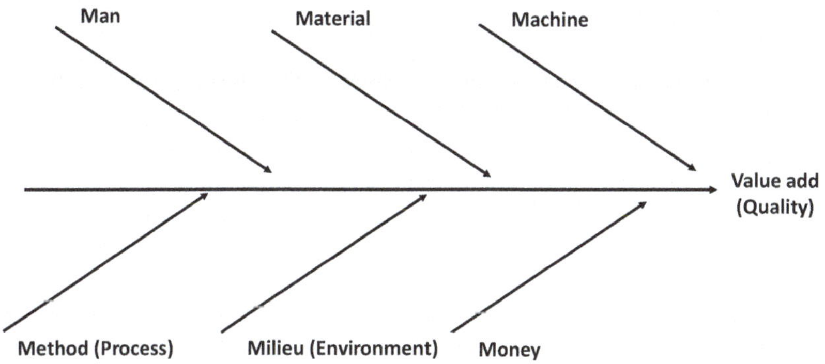

Fig. 4.3 Ishikawa diagram. (Source: Author's source)

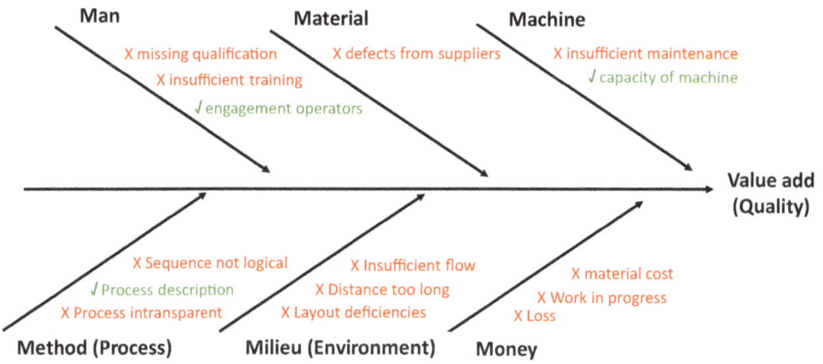

Fig. 4.4 Ishikawa diagram with waste and value-added. (Source: Author´ source)

4.3 Advantages and Disadvantages

The advantages and disadvantages are shown in the following paragraph.

Advantages

- Highly visual brainstorming tool which can spark further examples of root causes
- Quickly identify if the root cause is found multiple times in the same or different causal tree
- Allows one to see all causes simultaneously
- Good visualization for presenting issues to stakeholders

Disadvantages

- Complex defects might yield a lot of causes which might become visually cluttering.
- Interrelationships between causes are not easily identifiable.

4.4 5S System

5S is the name of a workplace organization method that uses a list of five Japanese words: seiri, seiton, seiso, seiketsu, and shitsuke. Transliterated into Roman script, they all start with the letter "S". 5S is used to stabilize, maintain, and improve the safest, best working environment, thus supporting sustainable QCD plus alpha. 5S is a systematic and structured workplace optimization, originally developed and used by Toyota. The objective is the identification and elimination of waste. In simple terms, the 5S methodology helps a workplace remove items that are no longer needed (sort), organize the items to optimize efficiency and flow (straighten), clean the area in order to more easily identify problems (shine), implement colour coding and labels to stay consistent with other areas (standardize), and develop behaviours that keep the workplace organized over the long term (sustain). 5S is a workplace organization method that uses a list of five Japanese words:

1. Seiri (整理)
2. Seiton (整頓)
3. Seisō (清掃)
4. Seiketsu (清潔)
5. Shitsuke (躾)

These five words can be translated as "sort", "set in order", "shine", "standardize", and "sustain". The 5S methodology describes how to organize a work space for efficiency and effectiveness by identifying and storing the items used, maintaining the area and items, and sustaining the new order. The decision-making process usually comes from a dialogue about standardization, which builds understanding among employees of how they should do the work.

In some quarters, 5S has become 6S, the sixth element being safety or self-discipline (Fig. 4.5).

The advantages of the 5S system are the following:

- Creation of transparent layout and processes
- Makes waste transparent
- Eliminates unnecessary activities
- Improves efficiency
- Increases safety
- Increases employee motivation and simplification of the work environment
- Ensuring that all materials are instantly available
- Ensuring that tools (screwdriver, devices)
- Ensuring that required (work procedures, work sequence, etc.) information is instantly available by visualization
- Reduction of waste

The first element in the 5S concept is the sorting (seiri). In this step it is important to distinguish between necessary and unnecessary things. Things in this context are

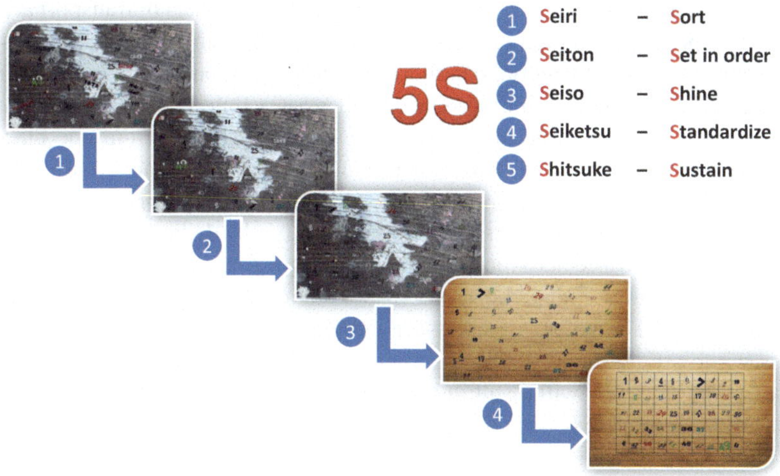

Fig. 4.5 5S system. (Source: Author's source)

materials, components, tools, gauges, information, things, and people. Unnecessary things must disappear. Removing these items which are not used in the working area may take a reasonable amount of time. Classification of all equipment and materials by frequency will help to decide if these items can be removed or not. The second step is the setting in order (seiton), so that the right item can be picked efficiently at the right time, which is easy to access for the operators. Alongside this step secures that only tools and information are available, which are needed fo the oprtation. Identification and allocation of materials, information, tools, and necessary things at fixed and visualized locations are important in this step. In the next and third step (seiso), it is mandatory to create a clean worksite without garbage, dirt, and dust, so problems can be more easily identified (leaks, spills, excess, damage, etc.). In the fourth step (seiketsu), standards for a neat, clean workplace and operations will be set up through visual management. In the fifth and last stage (shitsuke), it is important to create the environment, patterns, management style, and behaviours that secure that the established standards are executed over the long-term. The concept of 5S makes sure that the lean and efficient workplace organization is the key for the successful achievement of superior quality and results in operations and production (Helmold and Terry 2016a, b).

4.5 Seven Types of Waste in Operations

4.5.1 Transportation

Excess transportation is a significant waste because the time, manpower, energy, efforts, and resources required to move items are something the customer does not care and does not want to pay (Ohno 1990). Examples of wastes of transport are the transport of product from one functional area such as pressing to another area such as welding or the use of material handling devices to move batches of material from one machine to another within a work cell. It wastes time because operators are dedicating the available time of the work day to moving items from one place to another. It wastes energy and resources in that employee for time could be better utilized and because some tools used for transportation (forklifts, trucks, pallet jacks) consume energy like electricity or propane. Also, by dedicating machines and operators´ time to waste activities, they are no longer free and available to take on value-added activities. Figure 4.6 shows transportation waste. Reasons can be insufficient layouts and long distances between individual operations. The consequences of this waste are the increased time requirements and the decreased productivity. Decreased productivity will result in higher operating cost and can harm the profitability of the enterprise (Liker 2004).

4.5.2 Inventory

Inventory consists of excessive material of finished goods, semi-finished goods, or raw material. Finished goods inventory is generally the most expensive inventory as it has labour and other overhead attached to it along with the cost of material consumed during production. In order to reduce this inventory, process improvements and a higher accuracy in forecasting customer requirements are required. Inventory waste refers to the waste produced by unprocessed inventory. This includes the waste of storage, the waste of capital tied up in unprocessed inventory, the waste of

1. Transportation

Definition	Possible reasons
• Unnecessary transport of material • Transport is a necessary type of waste however it should be reduced to a minimum	• Insufficient arrangement of needed material and devices • Physical distance between material delivery and usage • Interim storage of material (buffer)
Consequences	**Examples**

• Additional space for transport
• Blocking of capacity due to additional logistic effort
• Possible damage of products
	• Long or additional transport of:
	  • Raw material
	  • Finished goods
	  • Tools and devices

Fig. 4.6 Transportation

2. Inventory

Definition

- More material than needed according to planning in terms of:
  - Raw material
  - Semi-finished parts
  - Work in progress (WIP)
  - Finished goods

Possible reasons

- Problems regarding planning and logistic processes
- Bad supplier delivery performance and quality
- High product variety

Consequences

- Capital costs
- Double handling, possible damages based on double handling, rework
- Genuine problems won't be discovered and therefore not solved
- Search effort
- Scrap

Examples

- Overfilled warehouses
- Overfilled place in production areas
- Buffer stocks in producton
- Crammed corridors
- Crammed desks

Fig. 4.7 Inventory

transporting the inventory, the containers used to hold inventory, the lighting of the storage space, etc. Moreover, having excess inventory can hide the original wastes of producing said inventory. The environmental impacts of inventory waste are packaging, deterioration or damage to work in process, additional materials to replace damaged or obsolete inventory, and the energy to light, as well as either heat or cool, inventory space. Figure 4.7 displays the definition, reasons, consequences, and examples for inventory. Inventory will have a negative impact on working capital and on cash flow, so that sophisticated production planning must focus on the optimum levels of inventory throughout the value chain and operations (Helmold and Terry 2016a, b).

4.5.3 Motion

Motion waste is the excessive movement of man, material, or machines within the work space. Motion waste will lead to higher cost as the productivity decreases. Another problem of motion is the necessity for more time and capacity in operations than actually required. A proper workflow analysis and value stream mapping help to minimize this waste. Figure 4.8 outlines the definition, possible reasons, consequences, and examples of this waste.

3. Motion

Definition	Possible reasons
• Every type of movement that doesn't directly serve value creation	• Inaccurate analysis of all workflows Inappropriate layout • Insufficient delivery of material and arrangement of tools
Consequences	**Examples**
• Decrease of productivity • Increase of lead time and capacity • Insufficient ergonomics	• Long ways between tools, material and product or machine • Missing material or tools

Fig. 4.8 Motion

4. Waiting

Definition	Possible reasons
• A period in which no activities take place. • The employee is forced to wait and can't fulfil any value added activities. During the holding period the product is waiting for processing	• Insufficiently synchronised material and information flows • Insufficient line balancing of all processes • Missing material or tools • Lack of documentation • Waiting for quality approval
Consequences	**Examples**
• Reduced productivity • Decreasing efficiency • Increased lead time • Increase of capacity • Decreased of employee motivation	• Waiting for material or tools e.g. crane • Quality employees are not available • Stopped processes due to missing resources (employees, defective machines, IT,...)

Fig. 4.9 Waiting

4.5.4 Waiting

Idle time of operators or other employees in operations and waiting for work to arrive or to be told what to do are a significant waste. Waiting or standstill times must be avoided as waiting results into reduced efficiency and productivity. Other outcomes are longer lead times and decreasing engagement and motivation of employees as illustrated in Fig. 4.9.

5. Overproduction

Definition	Possible reasons
• If more is produced than the internal or external customer needs	• Insufficient transparency of real demand • Production according to supposed optimal batch sizes • Instable processes • Early use of available capacity
Consequences	**Examples**
• Generation of inventory (warehouse, WIP) • Additional use of space • Blocking of capacities (machines, employees) • Double handling, decrease of product quality	• A lot of material in front of machines or assembly lines • Crowded warehouses

Fig. 4.10 Overproduction

4.5.5 Overproduction

Overproduction waste is defined as producing too many products too early and in advance. That means that parts in a big quantity are existing inside operations management, even though these parts are not needed. Figure 4.10 displays possible reasons such as demand non-transparency or inadequate batch sizes. A consequence of this waste is that inventory increases drastically and that work-in-progress cost rises significantly.

4.5.6 Overprocessing

Overprocessing is related to all activities and processes in operations, which are more than the customer really needs. Figure 4.11 highlights possible reasons such as insufficient technology, bad design, inefficiencies, or unawareness of customer-specific requirements. Overprocessing refers to any component of the process of manufacture that is unnecessary. Painting an area that will never be seen and adding features that will not be used are examples of overprocessing. Essentially, it refers to adding more value than the customer requires. The environmental impact involves the excess of parts, labour, and raw materials consumed in production. Time, energy, and emissions are wasted when they are used to produce something that is unnecessary in a product; simplification and efficiency reduce these wastes and benefit the company and the environment.

6. Overprocessing

Definition	Possible reasons
• Process weakness in terms of sequence, content, technologies and resources	• Insufficient technology • Not the most efficient procedure for the process • Insufficient analysis and design of processes • Due to process problems the product requirements in the specification are higher than required by the customer
Consequences	**Examples**
• High production costs • Waste of material • Low efficiency • High need for resources (employee, machine, material)	• High tolerances • Wrong, faulty and not needed process steps • Not optimal utilisation of resources • Duplication of efforts

Fig. 4.11 Overprocessing

7. Defects

Definition	Possible reasons
• If right first time is not achieved	• Lack of machine and tool maintenance • Insufficiently trained employees • Product not according to customer requirements • Unstable or not standardized processes • No problem solving process established
Consequences	**Examples**
• Additional need for material, tools and capacity • Additional space for rework • Increase of quality employees and checks • Increase of lead time	• Increase of non-conformities • Retrofitting and repairing defect parts • Increased quantity of scrap • Supply issues due to bad quality

Fig. 4.12 Defects

4.5.7 Defects

Defects as shown in Fig. 4.12 refer to a product deviating from the standards of its design or from the customer's expectation. Defective products must be replaced; they require paperwork and human labour to process it; they might potentially lose customers; the resources put into the defective product are wasted because the

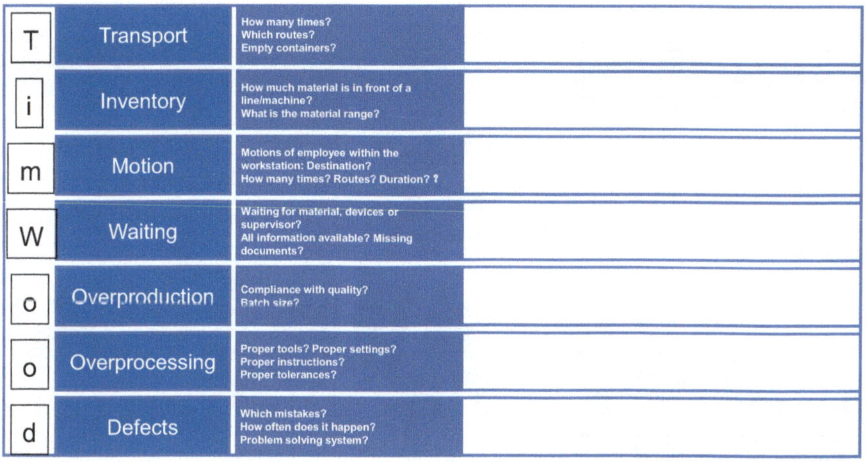

Fig. 4.13 TIMWOOD checklist

product is not used. Moreover, a defective product implies waste at other levels that may have led to the defect to begin with; making a more efficient production system reduces defects and increases the resources needed to address them in the first place. Environmental costs of defects are the raw materials consumed, the defective parts of the product requiring disposal or recycling (which wastes other resources involved in repurposing it), and the extra space required and increased energy use involved in dealing with the defects.

The checklist in Fig. 4.13 is the ideal tool to assess operations in terms of the seven wastes. It is a proven method for identifying waste in process and activities (Helmold and Terry 2016a, b).

4.6 Case Study: Bombardier in China

Bombardier is recognized as a successful foreign enterprise in the Chinese rail industry. Bombardier is also a specially qualified Western enterprise which supplies railway passenger trains (high-speed trains and intercity passenger trains), metro vehicles, monorail trains, APM systems, and metro vehicle maintenance/services. Bombardier Transportation in China has 6 joint ventures, 7 wholly foreign-owned enterprises, and around 7000 employees (Bombardier 2020).

A wide range of our rail transportation and aerospace products are currently in service in the Chinese market. In total, more than 30,000 rail vehicles, locomotives, bogies, and propulsion systems are in operation or on order in China, including more than 3500 high-speed train and intercity passenger train cars, 580 electric locomotives, over 2000 metro cars, and maintenance for 1600 metro cars as part of China's growing urban mass transit market. Bombardier is also supplying, or

Fig. 4.14 Bombardier Sifang Transportation China – final testing. (Source: Author's source)

has already supplied, APM systems to China's five largest cities: Beijing, Guangzhou, Shanghai, Shenzhen, and Hong Kong. In addition, Bombardier has supplied 104 tram cars for 2 other Chinese megacities (Nanjing/Suzhou) and in 2017 won its first monorail contract in China, for 240 cars. A total of over 14,000 Bombardier bogies are currently in use in China's mainline and urban mass transit vehicles, while Bombardier's propulsion and signalling equipment, largely supplied to third-party metro car builders, are in operation in more than 30 Chinese cities.

Figure 4.14 displays the assembly and testing line of high-speed trains in Bombardier Sifang Transportation. Figure 4.14 shows the visualization room of the International Procurement Office (IPO) in Shanghai. International purchasing offices or supplier management centres are part of the internationalization and change of corporate model in supplier management (Helmold 2014a, b). Multinational corporations such as Volkswagen, Daimler, Siemens, Bosch, or Bombardier have purchasing offices in regions such as China, India, or Eastern Europe, which offer savings potential or are geographically far removed from the parent company. Medium-sized partners expand through smaller offices or through collaboration with partners, purchasing offices or institutions such as the German centres in the metropolitan areas of China. (Helmold and Terry 2016a, b). In addition to offices, the German centres also offer contacts to government representatives or Chinese suppliers in order to make purchases from China (Helmold and Terry 2016a, b). In 2015, Deutsche Bahn opened an international purchasing office. Previously, the logistics division, DB Schenker, had successfully established itself in many locations over the years. In 2005, companies such as Bombardier

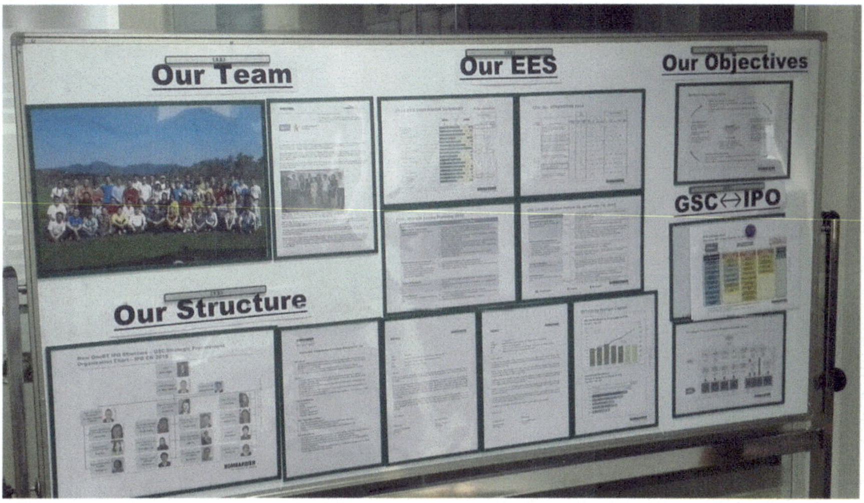

Fig. 4.15 Visualization at Bombardier Transportation – International Procurement Office. (Source: Author's source)

Transportation or IBM opened an international purchasing office in Shanghai, China (Bombardier Transportation 2016). In 2015, Deutsche Bahn decided to open a point-of-sale office in the same location. Developments show that it is advisable to establish an international purchasing office in China. Advantages can be outlined as follows:

- Proximity to markets with a high degree of product and know-how maturity, e.g. automotive industry or railway industry
- Establishing relationships with Chinese manufacturers and ensuring compliance with quality requirements
- Transfer of customer and production requirements to the suppliers
- Early involvement of suppliers in the product development process as well as joint development
- Exploitation of savings through direct purchasing as well as through the use of local pre- and semi-finished products in the production process of the suppliers
- Acquisition of own end products in domestic markets
- Proximity to other high maturity Asian markets, e.g. Japan or South Korea

Figure 4.15 depicts an example of the 5S concept in China at Zhongwang in Shenyang. The company changed in a very creative way the 5S philosophy into eight categories (8S) (Fig. 4.16).

Fig. 4.16 8S example in China. (Source: Author)

References

Bombardier. (2020). Retrieved 1 Feb 2020. https://rail.bombardier.com/en/about-us/worldwide-presence/china/en.html.

Helmold, M. (2014a). Erfahrungen aus der Bahnindustrie. Lieferantenmanagement in China. Beschaffung aktuell. 03/2014, 22–25.

Helmold, M. (2014b). *Establishing a best-practice model of supplier relationship management (SRM) in multinational companies in the European transportation industry*. Berlin: Wissenschaftlicher Verlag.

Helmold, M., & Terry, B. (2016a). Lieferantenmanagement 2030. In *Sicherung der Wettbewerbsfähigkeit durch wertfokussierte Lieferantenbeziehungen*. Wiesbaden: Springer Verlag.

Helmold, M., & Terry, B. (2016b). *Global sourcing and supply management excellence in China*. Singapore: Springer.

Liker, J. K. (2004). *The Toyota way*. Madison: McGraw-Hill.

Lean Management as Part of the Corporate Strategy

5

When you're dying of thirst, it is too late to think about digging a well.

Japanese say

5.1 Definition of Strategic Management

Lean management must be the integral part of the corporate strategy (Helmold, Dathe, and Hummel 2019). Strategic management is a framework that is dealing with recognizing and making the important changes towards its lean mission and vision by using resources and assets in the most efficient way (Helmold and Samara 2019). It is a framework which links strategic planning and decision-making with the everyday business of operational administration. Strategic management is very important for an organization's long-term success, which is making companies able to compete in a hostile and competitive environment (Johnson and Scholes 1997). Translation of strategic management plans into practice is the most important aspect of the planning itself in any organization. Strategic and lean plans can include actions like entering new markets, global sourcing, make-or-buy strategies, deployment of new products or services, centralization or decentralization of activities, or aligning leadership and resources as outlined by various authors (Johnson and Scholes 1997; Mintzberg et al. 1995; Porter 1980; Helmold et al. 2019).

Porter is best known for his strategic frameworks and concepts in his paper, which was published in 1980 (Porter 1980). The five forces model (industry analysis) has five elements that can be utilized to assess the attractiveness and competitive situation of the industry. The five elements are:

1. Rivalry among competitors
2. Bargaining power of suppliers
3. Bargaining power of buyers

M. Helmold, *Lean Management and Kaizen*, Management for Professionals,
https://doi.org/10.1007/978-3-030-46981-8_5

4. Threat of new market entrants
5. Threat of new substitutes

Moreover, the generic strategies differentiation and cost leadership are a good method to define in which direction a company should go to increase profitability and to acquire a competitive advantage (Porter 1980, 1985; Helmold et al. 2019). Mintzberg provides five definitions of strategy, plan, ploy, pattern, position, and perspective (Mintzberg,Quinn, and Goshal 1995). Firstly, strategy is always a plan. A plan integrates intended actions activities based on previous assessment of the situation. Secondly, as plan, a strategy can be a ploy too, really just a specific manoeuvre intended to outwit an opponent or competitor. If strategies can be intended (whether as general plans or specific ploys), they can also be realized. In other words, defining strategy as plan is not sufficient; we also need a definition that encompasses the resulting behaviour. Thirdly, strategy is a pattern. The definitions of strategy as plan and pattern can be quite independent of one another. Plans may go unrealized, while patterns may appear without preconception. Plans are intended strategy, whereas patterns are the realized strategy. Fourthly, strategy is a perspective. A perspective is not just of a chosen position, but consists of an ingrained way of perceiving the world (Mintzberg, Quinn, and Goshal 1995).

5.2 Strategic Triangle

The process of strategic management cycle is a process with three elements as outlined in Fig. 5.1 (strategic triangle or strategic cycle) (Johnson and Scholes 1997). The three steps are (1) the strategic analysis, (2) the strategic choice, and (3) the

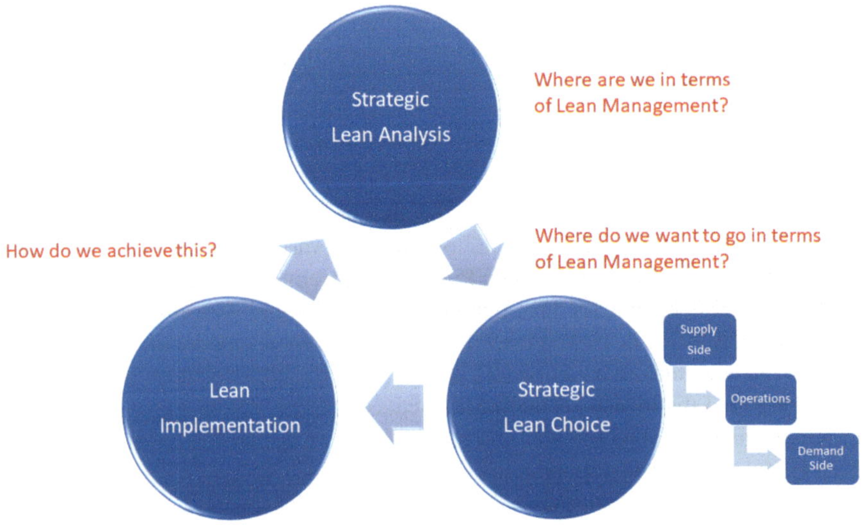

Fig. 5.1 Strategic triangle. (Source: Compiled by the author, adopted from Johnson and Scholes (1997))

strategic implementation and will be described in the following sections. The triangle is raising the following questions:

1. Where are we in terms of lean management?
2. Where do we want to go?
3. How do we achieve this?

5.3 Strategic Analysis

The strategic analysis of an organization is about understanding the strategic position of the organization in terms of lean management. This stage requires a profound analysis where the organization stands in terms of lean management tools and processes (Johnson and Scholes 1997). The existing competencies and resources of the organization need to be assessed to determine if there are any opportunities to be gained from these and to determine if they need to be enhanced in order to pursue strategic objectives and goals (Johnson and Scholes 1997). The major stakeholders which influence the organization and the opinions or viewpoints must be taken into account as the purpose of all of the strategic analysis is to define the potential future direction of the organization. The purpose of this phase (strategic analysis) is to create a suitable starting position and to understand the key influences on the present and future state of the organization and what opportunities are afforded by the environment and the competencies of the organization Johnson and Scholes 1997). Assessing the strategic position consists of evaluating the following elements as shown in Table 5.1.

Since strategy is concerned with the position a business takes in relation to its environment, an understanding of the environment's effects on an organization is of central importance to the strategic analysis. The historical and environmental effects on the business must be considered, as well as the present effects and the expected changes in environmental variables. The analysis of the environment can be done via the macro and micro analysis (PESTEL, Porter's five forces).

Additionally, strengths, weaknesses, opportunities, and threats (SWOT) complete the assessment of the environment. This step is a major task because the range of environmental variables is so great. Another area of the strategic analysis is the

Table 5.1 Elements in the strategic analysis

Strategic analysis of elements	Strategic tool
Environment (e.g. markets, regulations, political impacts)	PESTEL analysis (macro)
Industry and competition (e.g. rivalry in industry)	Industry analysis (micro)
Internal strengths and weaknesses, external threats and opportunities	SWOT analysis (internal)
Cultures and beliefs	Cultural analysis
Strategic capabilities and competencies	Benchmarking analysis
Expectation of stakeholders	Stakeholder analysis

Source: Author's own table

evaluation of the strategic capability of an organization and where it is able to achieve a competitive advantage. Considering the resource areas of a business such as its physical plant, its management, its financial structure, and its products may identify these strengths and weaknesses (Johnson and Scholes 1997).

The expectations of stakeholders are important because they will affect what will be seen as acceptable in terms of the strategies advanced by management. Stakeholders can be defined as people or groups inside or outside the organization, with an interest in the activities of the organization. A typical list of stakeholders for a large company would include shareholders, banks, employees, managers, customers, suppliers, government, and society. Culture affects the interpretation of the environmental and resource influences (Johnson and Scholes 1997).

5.4 Strategic Choice

Strategic choice typically follows strategic analysis. Strategic choice involves a whole process through which a decision is taken to choose a particular option from various alternatives. There can be various methods through which the final choice can be selected upon. Managers and decision-makers keep both the external and internal environment in mind before narrowing it down to one. It is based upon the following three elements: first, the generation of strategic options, e.g. growth, acquisition, diversification, or concentration; second, the evaluation of the options to assess their relative merits and feasibility; and, third, the selection of the strategy or option that the organization will pursue. There could be more than one strategy chosen, but there is a chance of an inherent danger or disadvantage to any choice made. Although there are techniques for evaluating specific options, the selection is often subjective and likely to be influenced by the values of managers and other groups with an interest in the organization (Helmold et al. 2020) (Fig. 5.2).

5.5 Strategic Implementation

5.5.1 Assessment of Suitability, Acceptability, and Feasibility

Strategic implementation is concerned with the translation of the selected strategy into action (Johnson and Scholes 1997). The ways in which strategies are implemented are described as the strategic architecture or framework of the organization (Johnson and Scholes 1997). Successful implementation of the chosen strategy will be dependent on several factors such as stakeholder's expectations, the employees, the company culture, the will to change, and the cooperation within the organization. These elements and how the management and employees work together to adopt the new plan will decide about how successful the strategy implementation is. The available skills and/or the ability to develop new skills when required for the planned change and issues like the structural reorganization and resulting cultural disturbance would also affect success. Resource availability and planning for the

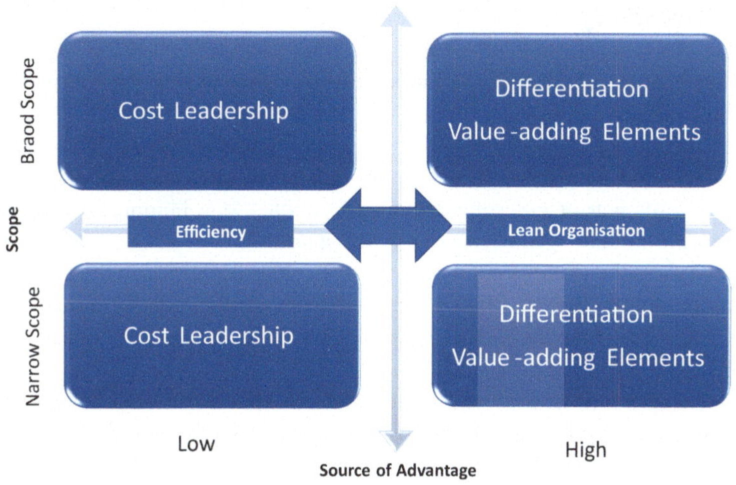

Fig. 5.2 Generic strategies. (Source: Author's own figure, adopted from Porter (1985))

utilization of such resources need to be addressed as part of the implementation plan. The entire process necessitates the management of strategic change and will concern handling both hard and soft factors of the organization, i.e. structure and systems and culture and motivation, etc. Implementing a strategy has three elements.

- Organizational structure and layout: Where and how should the organization split into European, US, and Asian divisions? How autonomous should divisions be? What parenting style should be applied?
- Resources: Enabling an organization's resources should support the chosen strategy: What are the appropriate human and non-human resources? What assets need to be acquired?
- Change management: Most strategic planning and implementation will involve change, so managing change, in particular employees' fears and resistance, is crucial

Johnson and Scholes argue that for a strategy to be successful, it must satisfy three criteria (Johnson and Scholes 1997). These criteria can be applied to any strategy decision such as the competitive strategies, growth strategies, or development strategies:

1. Suitability – whether the options are adequate responses to the firm's assessment of its strategic position
2. Acceptability – considers whether the options meet and are consistent with the firm's objectives and are acceptable to the stakeholders
3. Feasibility – assesses whether the organization has the resources it needs to carry out the strategy

5.5.2 Suitability

Suitability is a useful criterion for screening strategies, asking the following questions about strategic options:

- Does the strategy exploit the company strengths, such as providing work for skilled craftsmen or environmental opportunities, e.g. helping to establish the organization in new growth sectors of the market?
- How far does the strategy overcome the difficulties identified in the analysis? For example, is the strategy likely to improve the organization's competitive position, solve the company's liquidity problems, or decrease dependence on a particular supplier?
- Does the option fit in with the organization's purposes? For example, would the strategy achieve profit targets or growth expectations, or would it retain control for an owner-manager?

5.5.3 Acceptability

Acceptability is essentially about assessing risk and return and is strongly related to expectations of stakeholders. The issue of "acceptable to whom?" thus requires the analysis to be thought through carefully. Some of the questions that will help identify the likely consequences of any strategy are as follows:

- How will the strategy impact shareholder wealth? Assessing this could involve calculations relating to profitability, e.g. net present value (NPV).
- How will the organization perform in profitability terms? The parallel in the public sector would be cost/benefit assessment.
- How will the financial risk (e.g. liquidity) change?
- What effect will it have on capital structure (gearing or share ownership)?
- Will the function of any department, group, or individual change significantly?
- Will the organization's relationship with outside stakeholders, e.g. suppliers, government, unions, and customers, need to change?
- Will the strategy be acceptable in the organization's environment, e.g. higher levels of noise?

5.5.4 Feasibility

Assesses whether the organization has the resources it needs to carry out the strategy. Factors that should be considered can be summarized under the M-word model.

- Machinery. What demands will the strategy make on production? Do we have sufficient spare capacity? Do we need new production systems to give lower cost/better quality/more flexibility/etc.?
- Management. Is existing management sufficiently skilled to carry out the strategy?

- Money. How much finance is needed and when? Can we raise this? Is the cash flow feasible?
- Manpower. What demands will the strategy make on human resources? How many employees are needed, and what skills will they need and when do we need them? Do we already have the right people or is there a gap? Can the gap be filled by recruitment, retraining, etc.?
- Markets. Is our existing brand name strong enough for the strategy to work? Will new brand names have to be established? What market share is needed for success – how quickly can this be achieved?
- Materials. What demands will the strategy make on our relationships with suppliers? Are changes in quality needed?
- Make-up. Is the existing organizational structure adequate, or will it have to be changed?

5.6 Strategic Pyramid

A useful tool for the translation of the corporate strategy and strategic objectives into negotiations is the strategic pyramid (Johnson and Scholes 1997). Strategy in this context is the long-term positioning as well as the decision of the enterprise and which business fields and which strategies to choose. Strategy is therefore "the fundamental, long-term direction of three to five years and organization of a company in order to gain competitive advantages in a changing environment through the use of resources and competencies and to realize the long-term goals of the stakeholders" (Johnson and Scholes 1997) (Fig. 5.3).

5.6.1 Lean Mission and Vision

Enterprises must manifest in their strategy to strive for lean excellence (Helmold and Samara 2019). The mission is the starting point of the strategic pyramid. The mission statement of an enterprise is the long-term purpose of the company and the strategic direction as defined by Johnson and Scholes (1997). The vision or strategic intent describes more specifically what an organization aims to achieve and the long-term aspirations (Johnson and Scholes 1997).

Mission example: Become a lean enterprise of excellence on a global basis

Vision example: Become the world-leading company in lean in the industry in the next 5 years

5.6.2 Qualitative and Quantitative Lean Goals and Objectives

The mission and vision are followed by generic goals and specific objectives. Generic goals are not quantified and more general, but specific objectives are quantified and specific (Helmold et al. 2019). The strategists Johnson and Scholes distinguish in longer-term and generic (English: goals) as well as shorter and quantified

Fig. 5.3 Strategic pyramid. (Source: Author's own figure)

objectives (English: objectives) for the company (Johnson and Scholes 1997). Quantified goals can include sales, financial, quality, logistics, cost, and alpha goals.

Goal example: Increase and improve quality, reduce cost, and provide productivity improvements between 30 and 40 percent within the next 3 years.

Objectives example: Quantification of the generic aims (goals)

5.6.3 Core Competencies

The next level in the strategic pyramid is the identification of core competencies. Core competencies are those competencies which allow companies to gain a superior or competitive advantage and that are very difficult for your competitors to emulate (Johnson and Scholes 1997). These describe the resources, skills, knowledge, or any other features that lead to a competitive advantage. Core competencies must be perceived by customers and clients (Helmold et al. 2020).

Example: Create lean academy and lean culture.

5.6.4 Strategies

After defining mission, vision, goals, and core competencies, the elements must be translated into strategic objectives and key performance indicators (KPIs). The long-term implementation of these elements is defined as the formulation of strategic objectives and important for the negotiations (Helmold et al. 2019). In implementing the strategic goals, negotiations will take place with many stakeholders (Helmold et al. 2020). Become a lean differentiator by answering customer demands:

reduce operating cost by 25 percent in 12 months from now, and increase customer satisfaction by 10 percent.

5.6.5 Strategic Architecture

In addition to buildings, machines, plants, offices, resources, or employees, the infrastructure in the sense of strategic management also includes knowledge and innovations of the company that ensure long-term success (Helmold et al. 2019). This requires facilities, buildings, factories, or offices that represent the strategic infrastructure. In addition, however, other success criteria such as resources, knowledge, experts, name recognition, network, or innovations are of central importance.

5.6.6 Control and Execution

The final element of the strategic pyramid is the performance control (control and execution) and a target-performance comparison. A suitable tool for this step is the Balanced Scorecard (BSC) or an action plan. The instrument of the BSC was already developed in 1992 by the professors Norton and Kaplan. The BSC is an instrument in strategic management and includes four categories (Johnson and Scholes 1997):

1. Customer satisfaction
2. Financial category
3. Internal processes and improvements
4. Learning organization

In practice, it seems that companies are adapting or expanding the original four dimensions to their specific needs (Johnson and Scholes 1997).

Example: Establishing process and key performance indicators (KPIs) of monitoring improvements and successful execution of strategy. Creating scorecard and checking running time, sequence, weight, and other elements on a daily basis

5.7 Strategies Must Focus on Value Creation

Porter postulated three generic or broad alternative strategies which may be pursued as a response to the competitive pressures. They are termed generic strategies because they are broadly applicable to any industry or business. They are differentiation, cost leadership, and focus. A focus strategy may be further defined as cost focus, differentiation focus, or cost and differentiation focus. A differentiation strategy may be based on actual unique product features or the perception thereof, conveyed through the use of advertising and marketing tactics, in the eyes of the customers. Obviously, the product or service feature must be one the customer needs or desires. Moreover, such enhanced features and designs or advertising and

Fig. 5.4 Example of mission statement. (Source: Author's Source)

marketing will increase costs, and customers must be price-insensitive – willing to pay for the differentiated product or service. This willingness to pay for the differentiated product of service is what provides the company relief from competitive pressure, cost pressure specifically. Firms pursuing a cost leadership strategy must make lower production and distribution costs their priority (Johnson and Scholes 1997; Johnson et al. 2008). By keeping their cost lowers than those of their competitors, firms using cost leadership can still price their products up to the level of their competitors and still maintain higher gross profit margins. Alternatively, these firms can price their products lower than those of their competitors in the hope of achieving greater market share and sales volume at the expense of gross profit margins. A focus strategy is based on a particular market, customer, product, or geographic. A focus strategy is a concentrated, narrowly focused niche strategy. Figure 5.4 shows the example of a mission statement of Bombardier Transportation in China International Procurement Office (Fig. 5.5).

5.8 Case Study: Siemens Strategy

The company Siemens has outlined its mission, vision, goals, strategic objectives, core values, and cultural specifics in its strategy outline "Siemens Vision 2020" (Siemens 2019). The president and CEO, Joe Kaeser, outlines the key elements of the Siemens strategy for the coming years. He stresses that with the positioning along the electrification value chain, Siemens has know-how that extends from power generation to power transmission, power distribution, and smart grid to the efficient application of electrical energy. And with the outstanding strengths in

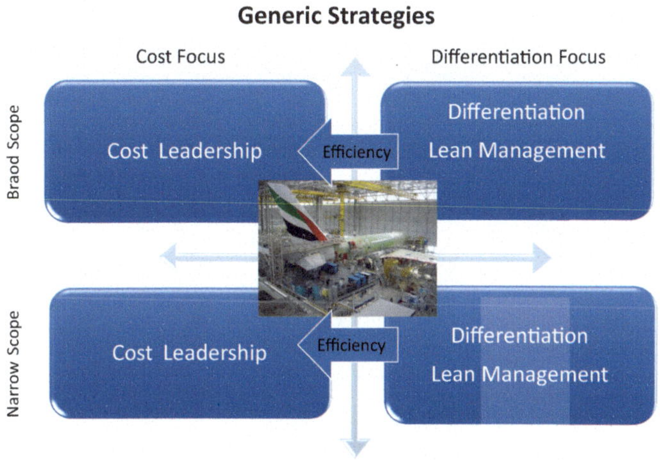

Fig. 5.5 Lean management as a strategy for differentiation and efficiency. (Source: Author's own figure)

automation, Kaeser confirms that Siemens is well equipped for the future and the age of digitalization. The Siemens Vision 2020 defines an entrepreneurial concept that will enable the enterprise to consistently occupy attractive growth fields, sustainably strengthen our core business and outpace, our competitors in efficiency and performance. All goals are focused on a long-term success (Siemens 2019). The mission of Siemens can be defined as "We make real what matters, by setting the benchmark, in the way we electrify, automate and digitalize the world around us. Ingenuity drives us and what we create is yours. Together we deliver" (Siemens 2019).

References

Helmold, M., et al. (2020). *Successful international negotiations. A practical guide for managing transactions and deals*. Heidelberg: Springer.

Helmold, M., Dathe, T. & Hummel., F. (2019). *Erfolgreiche Verhandlungen Best-in-Class Empfehlungen für den Verhandlungsdurchbruch*. Wiesbaden: Springer.

Helmold, M., & Samara, W. (2019). *Progress in Performance Management Industry Insights and Case Studies on Principles, Application Tools, and Practice*. Heidelberg: Springer.

Johnson, G., & Scholes, K. (1997). *Exploring corporate strategy. Text and cases* (4th ed.). London: Prentice Hall.

Johnson, G, Scholes, K., & Whittington, R. (2008). *Exploring corporate strategy*. 8th ed. FT Prentice Hall, p. 11–13, 224, 294.

Mintzberg, H., Quinn, J. B., & Ghoshal, S. (1995). *The strategy process. Revised European edition*. London: Prentice Hall.

Porter, M. E. (1980). *Competitive strategy: Techniques for analyzing industries and competitors*. New York: Free Press.

Porter, M. E. (1985). *Competitive advantage. Creating and sustaining superior performance*. New York: Free Press.

Siemens (2019). Siemens strategy. www.siemens.de.

Leadership and Empowerment

6

The Toyota style is not to create results by working hard. It is a system that says there is no limit to people's creativity. People don't go to Toyota to "work" they go there to "think".

Taiichi Ohno (1912–1990)

6.1 Leadership in Lean Management

Leadership is defined as the way of motivating and directing a group of people to jointly work towards achieving common goals and objectives (Helmold & Samara 2019; Fatma 2015). The leader is the person in the group that possesses the combination of personality and leadership skills that makes others want to follow his or her direction. Leadership implies formal and informal power distribution. The Tannenbaum-Schmidt Leadership Continuum is a model showing the relationship between the level of authority you use as a leader and the freedom this allows your team (Tannenbaum & Schmidt 2009). At one end of the continuum are managers who simply tell their employees what to do. At the other end of the continuum are managers who are completely hands off. As you move from one end of the continuum to the other, the level of freedom you give your team will increase, and your use of authority will decrease. Most managers and leaders will lie somewhere in the middle between these two extremes. The Leadership Continuum was developed by Robert Tannenbaum and Warren Schmidt in their 1958 *Harvard Business Review* (HBR) article: "How to Choose a Leadership Pattern". Tannenbaum was an organizational psychologist and Professor at the UCLA Anderson School of Management. Schmidt was also a psychologist who taught at the UCLA Anderson School of Management. Most leadership models ring-fence a leadership style and analyse it in isolation from other leadership styles. However, in practice, a single leadership style is not appropriate for all situations. Sometimes you might want to borrow elements

M. Helmold, *Lean Management and Kaizen*, Management for Professionals,
https://doi.org/10.1007/978-3-030-46981-8_6

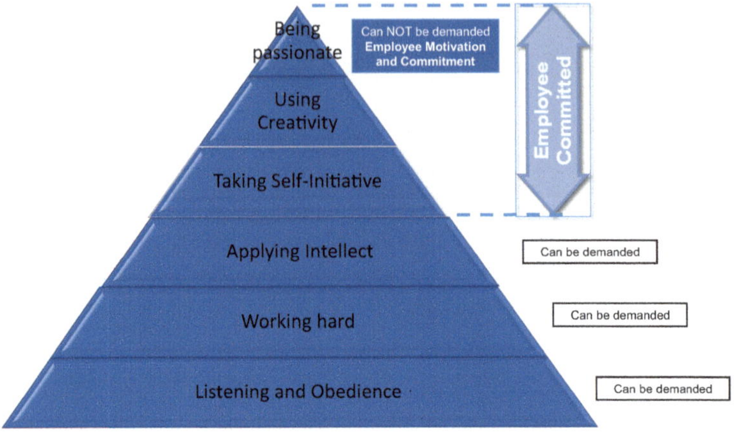

Fig. 6.1 Leadership in lean management focuses on employee motivation and commitment. (Source: Author's source)

of another leadership style to use with an individual within your team. Other times you might completely change your style if the situation requires it. Tannenbaum and Schmidt argued that there are certain questions to be considered when selecting a leadership style (Figs. 6.1 and 6.2):

- What is your preferred style?
- What are your values?
- What is your relationship with your team?
- Are they ready and enthusiastic to take responsibility?
- How important is the work being undertaken?
- How important or tight are deadlines?
- What is the organizational culture?

6.1.1 Tells

The leader that tells is an authoritarian leader. They tell their team what to do and expect them to do the work and job. This style is useful when you urgently need to turn around a department or business and also in situations where deadlines are critical. However, this extreme style can be frustrating for experienced subordinates as it takes no account of team members' welfare. Because of this, make sure you only use this style when the situation calls for it.

6.1.2 Sells

The leader that sells makes their decision and then explains the logic behind the decision to their team. The leader isn't looking for team input, but they are looking to ensure the team understands the rationale behind the decision. A key aspect of

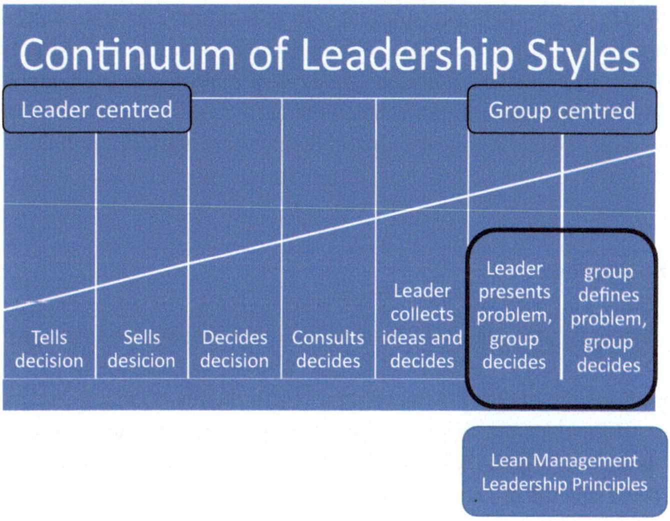

Fig. 6.2 Leadership styles. (Source: Author's source (adapted from Tannenbaum & Schmidt))

this approach is for the leader to explain how the decision will benefit the team. In this way, the team will see the manager as recognizing their importance.

6.1.3 Suggests

The leader that suggests makes their decision, explains the logic behind the decision, and then asks team members if they have any questions.

Through asking questions, the team can more fully understand the rationale behind the decision than the previous approaches. The leader isn't going to change their decision, but they do want the team to fully understand the rationale behind it.

6.1.4 Consults

The leader that consults presents their provisional decision to their team and invites comments, suggestions, and opinions. This is the first point on the continuum where the team's opinion can influence or even change the decision. The leader is still in control and the ultimate decision-maker, but open to any good ideas the team may have. With this style, the team feels they can influence the decision-making process. Once the leader has finished consulting with their team, their decision is finalized.

6.1.5 Joins

The leader who joins presents the problem to their team and then works with the team in a collaborative manner to make the decision as to how the problem is going to be solved. This point on the continuum differs from the previous four, as it is the first point the leader isn't presenting their decision. Instead, they are simply presenting the problem to be solved. This obviously will require plenty of input from the team, making this approach suitable when the team is very experienced or has specialist knowledge. Because this style involves greater input and influence form the team, it can lead to enhanced feelings of motivation and freedom.

6.1.6 Delegates

The leader that delegates asks their team to make the decision, within limits that the leader sets.

Although the team makes the decision, it is still the leader that is accountable for the outcome of the decision. It might seem very risky to let your team make a decision even though you'll be held accountable for the outcome. However, you can limit the risk by specifying constraints.

You should use this style only with very experienced teams.

6.1.7 Abdicates

The leader who abdicates lets the team decide what problems to solve and how to solve them.

Abdication is the total opposite of telling the team what to do using an autocratic style. Here the team must shape and identify the problem and analyse all the options available, before making a decision as to how to proceed. They will then implement the course of action without necessarily even running it by the leader. This style can be the most motivating but can be disastrous if it goes wrong. Because of this, you should only use this approach with very experienced and senior people. This style is often the way the executive boards of companies will run. Under the CEO, each of the division heads will have complete autonomy as to how they choose to execute the company's strategy.

6.2 Empowerment and Jidoka

A team is defined as group of people with common goals. A work or project team is a group of persons who are grouped according to process and/or geographical location who support each other. In the lean concept, it is important to empower teams as shown in Fig. 6.3. Whereas the conventional approach focuses on top-down decisions, the empowerment-focused approach utilizes the creativity and inputs from the team. Ideas are generated and collected from the team members, which independently decide which options to implement. The basis of this concept is that empowerment will promote ideas, creativity, and innovations from all team or project members. Employee empowerment must be implemented through organizational

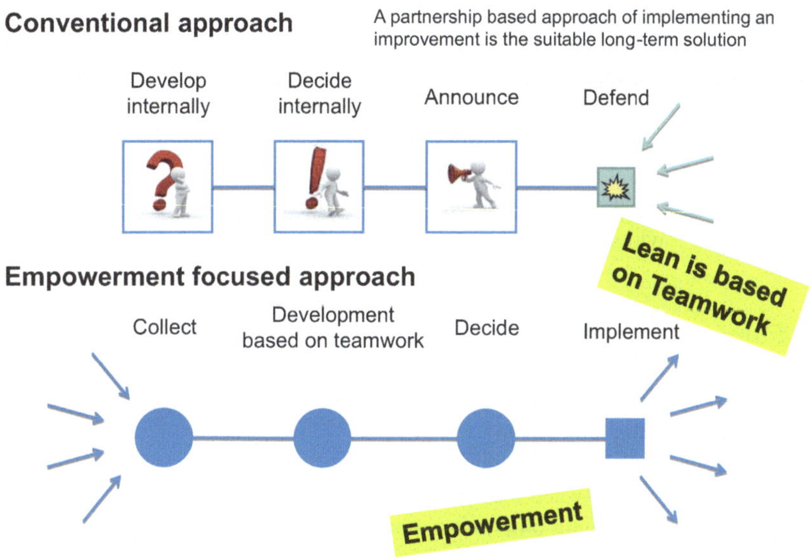

Fig. 6.3 Empowerment focused versus conventional approach. (Source: Author's source)

and cultural changes. This change must be starting with a top management, who is willing to trust employees with decisions regarding their work. When it comes to production, many modern companies still operate as they did in the early twentieth century, where the production employees are merely "the workers.

The lean concept of empowerment and stopping production to fix a problem found in production is called "jidoka" which means "getting it right the first time" rather than passing it on to the customer (next work station). Jidoka is a prime example of the lean philosophy of "quality at the source" which emphasizes that every production worker (and supplier) is responsible and empowered for providing quality material to their customer.

6.3 Autonomous Work Groups

Similar to an individual with autonomy at work, an autonomous work group is a team of employees granted autonomy or independence over the work they do within an organization.

6.4 Job Rotation

Job rotation is a management approach where employees are shifted between two or more assignments or jobs at regular intervals of time in order to expose them to all verticals of an organization. The process serves the purpose of both the management and the employees. Advantages and disadvantages of job rotation are given below.

Advantages of Job Rotation

- Reduces the monotony of work
- Broadens one's knowledge and skills
- Helps the management to explore the hidden talent of an individual
- Helps an individual to realize his own interest
- Helps in creating the right employee job fit
- Developing a wider range of experience

Disadvantages of Job Rotation

- Reduces uniformity of work
- Fear of performing another task effectively
- Frequent interruptions in the work
- Misunderstanding between the team members or union
- Difficulty in coping with other team members
- Fear of getting more tedious or a hectic work

The job rotation is beneficial for both the employer and the employee. The employer can identify the vertical where the employee is giving his best and can also place him in the position of a person who has left because of the retirement, transfer, termination, or any other reason.

6.5 Job Enlargement and Job Enrichment

Job enlargement is an increase in job tasks and responsibilities to make a position more challenging. It is a horizontal expansion, which means that the tasks added are at the same level as those in the current position. The job enrichment is the job design technique used to increase the satisfaction among the employees by delegating higher authority and responsibility to them and thereby enabling them to use their abilities to the fullest. Job enrichment will affect more the motivation, as the quality of work will be enriched to the employee (Fig. 6.4).

6.6 The Manager as the Coach of Employees

6.6.1 Case Study: BMW Quality Through Job Rotation

The BMW Group has more than 92,000 worldwide and centres them inside the middle of the corporate strategy. The human resource policy is with the Munich automakers firmly integrated in corporate policy and affects all strategic or structural decisions. Already since 1983, the company BMW applies an

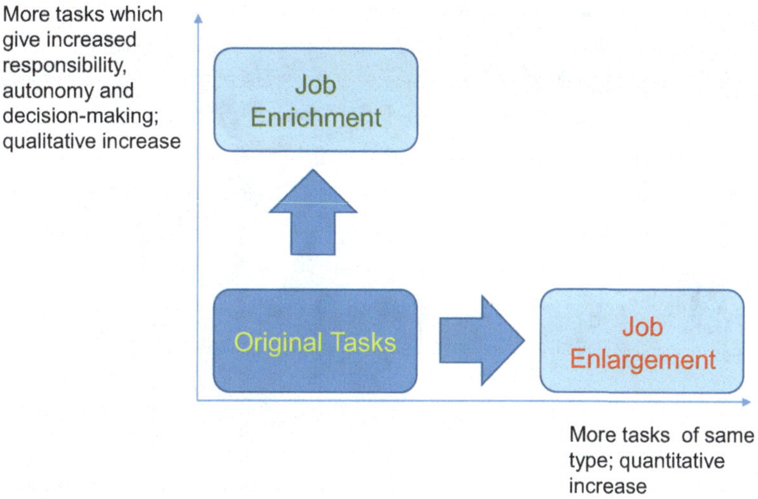

Fig. 6.4 Job enlargement and job enrichment. (Source: Author's source)

employee-oriented personnel policy. Present and future employees are not only a cost factor but a success factor for achieving long-term sustainable competitive advantages (BMW 2019). BMW not only introduced flexible working time models but also created new work structure with more freedom, thus using the employees in an optimal way. This way, the company left the traditional way and methods of the division of labour towards integrated working structures. Integration means in this context that project tasks and all processes are defined, divided, and fulfilled. This is done by leaving the traditional way of specialized functions and departments to a cross-functional project team, in which project teams are responsible for achieving the overall project results. For this change in human resources, it is mandatory to train not only hard skills (technical knowledge, etc.) but also soft and social skills (team skills, leadership, etc.). The acquisition of such new skills provides some variety and enrichment in the daily work and provides for each individual personal development opportunities, so that job rotation is possible. The application shows numerous exchange experiences and insights into a large range of work processes and jobs (BMW 2019). One example is that of Mr. Kroneder, previously trainer in the field of electronics, who rotated his job with Mr. Hillerbrand, maintenance for electronics in the vehicle final assembly and vice versa. The aim is to create a new technical trainer with assembly line experience and to enable a fully qualified trainer to apply the knowledge at the shop floor and to help workers at the assembly line area to develop in this job rotation program. This job rotation was executed for a period of 6 months. Because the exchange between production and training is very positive proves it is planned to train two instructors annually between 6 months and a whole year to offer this opportunity (BMW 2019) (Fig. 6.5).

Fig. 6.5 BMW production. (Source: Author's source)

References

BMW (2019). Jobrotation bei der BMW Group. Retrieved 4 Nov 2019. https://www.press.bmwgroup.com/deutschland/article/detail/T0005760DE/jobrotation-bei-der-bmw-group?language=de.

Fatma, P. (2015). The effect of organizational culture on implementing and sustaining lean processes. *Journal of Manufacturing Technology Management, 26*(5), 725–743.

Helmold, M., & Samara, W. (2019). *Progress in performance management. Industry insights and case studies on principles, application tools, and practice. Management for professionals.* Heidelberg: Springer.

Tannenbaum, R., & Schmidt, W. H. (2009). *How to choose a leadership pattern (Harvard business review classics).* Harvard Business Press: Harvard.

7 Lean Management in Operations

Get closer than ever to your customers. So close that you tell them what they need well before they realize it themselves.

Steve Jobs

7.1 Operations Management: Gemba, Gembutsu, and Genchi

Operations management was previously called production management, clearly showing its origins in manufacturing. Operations management is the area of management concerned with designing and controlling the process of production and redesigning business operations in the production of goods or services. Operations management is the transformation of goods and services. It involves the responsibility of ensuring that all company activities and business operations are most efficient in terms of using as few resources as needed and effective in terms of meeting customer requirements (James et al. 1997). It is part of the value chain and in between the supply side (procurement of goods) and the demand side (marketing and sales) as shown in Fig. 7.1. Operations management is primarily concerned with planning, organizing, and supervising in the contexts of production, manufacturing, or the provision of services (Helmold and Terry 2016).

Operations is concerned with managing an entire production system which is the process that converts inputs (in the forms of raw material, labour, energy, and resources) into outputs (in the form of goods and/or services) as an asset or delivers a product or services. Operations produce products, manage quality, and create service. Operations management covers sectors like banking systems, hospitals, companies, working with suppliers, customers, and using technology. Operations are one of the major functions in an organization along with supply chains, marketing, finance, and human resources. The operations function requires management of

M. Helmold, *Lean Management and Kaizen*, Management for Professionals,
https://doi.org/10.1007/978-3-030-46981-8_7

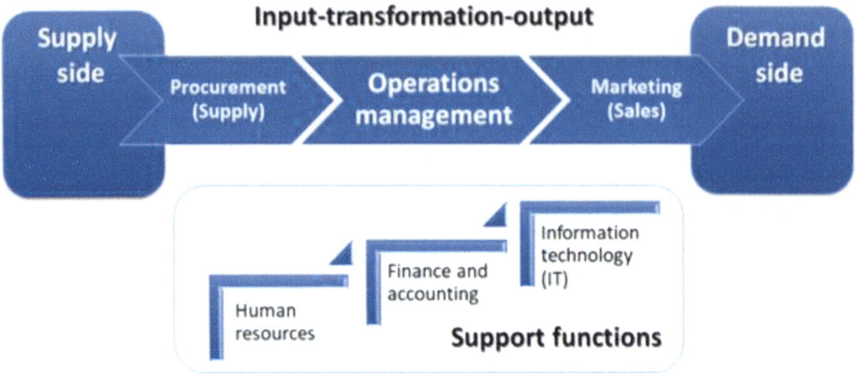

Fig. 7.1 Operations management as part of the value chain. (Source: Marc Helmold)

Objectives	Criteria
1. Right part	• Needed part
2. Right time	• Now
3. Right place	• Here
4. Right quantity	• One piece
5. Right quality	• Zero defect
6. Right employee	• Qualification
7. Right price	• Optimal cost

Fig. 7.2 7R principle in operations management

both the strategic and day-to-day production of goods and services. Operations management involves the production, planning, organizing, and supervising processes of products or services and targets to meet customer demands by delivering the right product or service at the right quality, quantity, time, and place with right people at the right cost. This principle is called the 7R principle and targets the optimal satisfaction of the goal in the operations function. Figure. 7.2 highlights the 7R principle with objectives and criteria behind the objectives (Helmold and Terry 2016).

7.2 Gemba, Gembutsu, and Genchi: Right Place of Happening

Gemba (現場) is also a Japanese term meaning “the real place”. Japanese detectives call the crime scene gemba, and Japanese TV reporters may refer to themselves as reporting from gemba. In business, gemba refers to the place where value is created; in manufacturing the gemba is the factory floor. It can be any “site” such as a construction site, sales floor, or where the service provider interacts directly with the customer. In lean production and supply management, the idea of gemba is that the problems are visible, and the best improvement ideas will come from going to the gemba. The gemba walk, much like management walk around (MWA), is an activity that takes management to the front lines to look for waste and opportunities to practice gemba kaizen, or practical shop floor improvement. In quality management, gemba means the manufacturing floor and the idea is that if a problem occurs, the engineers must go there to understand the full impact of the problem, gathering data from all sources. Unlike focus groups and surveys, gemba visits are not scripted or bound by what one wants to ask. Glenn Mazur introduced this term into quality function and supply management department (QFD, a quality system for new products where manufacturing has not begun) to mean the customer's place of business or lifestyle. The idea is that to be customer-driven, one must go to the customer's gemba to understand his problems and opportunities, using all one's senses to gather and process data.

Gembutsu (現地現物) is a Japanese word meaning "real thing". It is one of the components of the "three reals" meaning go to the real place (gemba) to see the real thing (gembutsu) and collect the real facts (genjitsu). This term simply means that there is no substitute for seeing something with one's own eyes.

Genchi (現地) is the Japanese principle of going to and directly observing a location and its conditions in order to understand and solve any problems faster and more effectively. The phrase literally translated means "go and see for yourself" and is a part of the Toyota Way philosophy (Fig. 7.3).

7.3 Muda, Muri, and Mura

In contrast to the traditional paradigm, the objectives of lean production are based on a reduction of throughput times and the elimination of non-value-adding activities. These activities are waste or so called MUDA (Japanese: 無駄). Both concepts, the traditional and the lean concept, are directed towards customer satisfaction. Nevertheless, the lean concept's foundation is based on the optimal reaction capability and not based on inventories or waste. Inventories increase the cost of capital and have negative impacts on the shareholder value, whereas short cycle times lead to small inventories. Lean manufacturing or lean production, often simply "lean", is a systematic method for the elimination of waste ("muda") within a manufacturing system. Lean also takes into account waste created through overburden ("muri") and waste created through unevenness in workloads ("mura"). Working from the perspective of the client who consumes a product or service, "value" is any action or process that a customer would be willing to pay for. Essentially, lean is centred on making obvious what adds value by reducing everything else. Lean manufacturing is a management philosophy derived mostly from the Toyota Production System (TPS) (hence the term Toyotism is also prevalent) and identified as "lean" only in the 1990s. TPS is renowned for its focus on reduction of the original Toyota seven wastes to improve overall customer value, but there are varying perspectives on how

Fig. 7.3 Bombardier Sifang Transportation: Dr. M. Helmold and B. Lannoye. (Source: Author's source)

this is best achieved. The steady growth of Toyota, from a small company to the world's largest automaker, has focused attention on how it has achieved this success. There are three MUs including MUDA that support the elimination of waste within the philosophy of Toyota. In parallel to MUDA (Japanese: 無駄), there are MURA (Japanese: 無ら) and MURI (Japanese = 無理) which are the ground theory for the TPS. MURA means "in balance", MURI "overutilization". While certain capacities are too scarce (bottleneck), there are other resources significantly below their capacity limits. The main objective of procurement and a strategic supplier management is to apply the JIT principle to the suppliers. Value-adding activities have to be rolled out to all suppliers from raw material to module and keiretsu suppliers. The keiretsu supplier is the closest relationship and connection to a supplier (Japanese: 系列子会社). Keiretsu is an integration of suppliers into the own organization and system; there is in few cases partial ownership involved. There are four pillars for the lean production system. These are the integral parts of a lean production and JIT system. The four pillars consist of the flow, the tact, pull, and zero-defect principle, which have to be introduced simultaneously. In the sense of an optimized supply chain, it is a fundamental activity to implement these four principles towards all areas. Practical examples by Porsche Consulting show that the introduction of the TPS led to radical improvements in terms of errors and defects per car (quality), serial completion time (cost and productivity), and inventory (logistics and delivery). The study reveals that the reduction of defects per car was reduced by 63 percent. The throughput time could be improved by more than 53 percent. This caused a positive situation of inventory by 50 percent. In the JIT approach, it is important that the right part comes in the right quantity in the right quality at the right time to the right place as shown in the 7R principle. This principle focuses on a zero defect as shown in the next figure. This principle was defined in the previous chapters as part of the objectives. The principles can be regarded as obtaining the right parts at the right quality and at the right time. This has to be in line with the right quantity in the right place by the right people at the right price (Helmold and Terry 2016).

7.4 Heijunka

Heijunka (平準化) is a Japanese word that means "levelling". When implemented correctly, heijunka elegantly – and without haste – helps organizations meet demand while reducing wastes in production and interpersonal processes. The two main objectives are the standardization of operations and the capability of flexible production of alternate derivatives on the same line. Toyota defines heijunka as the overall levelling, in the production schedule, of the volume and variety of items produced in given time periods and adds that it is a prerequisite for just-in-time delivery (Helmold and Samara 2019).

Heijunka allows you to level your production in both volume and product diversity. Lean facilities that have implemented heijunka don't base their production off the actual flow of customer orders. Instead, the company will use the heijunka methodology to calculate the total volume of orders place in a specific time frame and level them out. This allows the facility to produce the same amount and mix each day, without the ebbs and flows of demand cycles (Bertagnolli 2018).

Balancing your workflow has many benefits to your organization. For instance, if you have an above-average week of orders, followed by a below-average week, you end up paying overtime the first week and sending employees home the following. This is waste in the simplest form that could have been avoided with heijunka.

7.5 Poka-Yoke

Poka-yoke (ポカヨケ) is a Japanese term that means "mistake-proofing". A poka-yoke is any mechanism in a lean concept a process that helps an equipment operator avoid (yokeru) mistakes (poka). Its purpose is to eliminate product defects by preventing, correcting, or drawing attention to human or other errors as they occur. The concept was formalized, and the term adopted, by Shigeo Shingo as part of the TPS. It was originally described as baka-yoke, but as this means "fool-proofing" (or "idiot-proofing"), the name was changed to the milder poka-yoke.

7.6 Jidoka

By definition, jidoka (自働化) is a lean method that is widely adopted in manufacturing and product development. Also known as autonomation, it is a simple way of protecting your company from delivering products of low quality or defects to your customers while trying to keep up your takt time. Jidoka can be defined as automation with human touch.

7.7 Chaku Chaku Line

Chaku Chaku is a way to operate a semiautomated manufacturing line. One or more workers walk around the line, add parts to the processes, and then start the process. While the process works on the part automatically, the worker adds the next part to the next process, and so on. The word "Chaku Chaku" comes from Japanese. It can mean either "Load, Load" (着々), or it can simply be the sound the machine makes while unloading (ちゃくちゃく), similar to "Clack-Clack".

The basic principle of the Chaku Chaku line is very simple. The worker moves around the line from process to process and only loads the parts into the machine. After loading the part, the worker starts the machine and moves to the next process. At the end of the line, the worker starts again from the beginning (Fig. 7.4).

7.8 Case Study: Mazda Lean Operation

Mazda Motor Corporation is based in Hiroshima (Japan) and employees about 50,000 people. Mazda is dedicated to developing vehicles that are distinctive and innovative, using the latest and most advanced technologies to satisfy the diverse needs of customers worldwide. To accomplish this, Mazda created a global R&D network with operations in Japan, the USA, Germany, and China (Wykowski 2019). The corporate vision is: "We love cars and want people to enjoy fulfilling lives

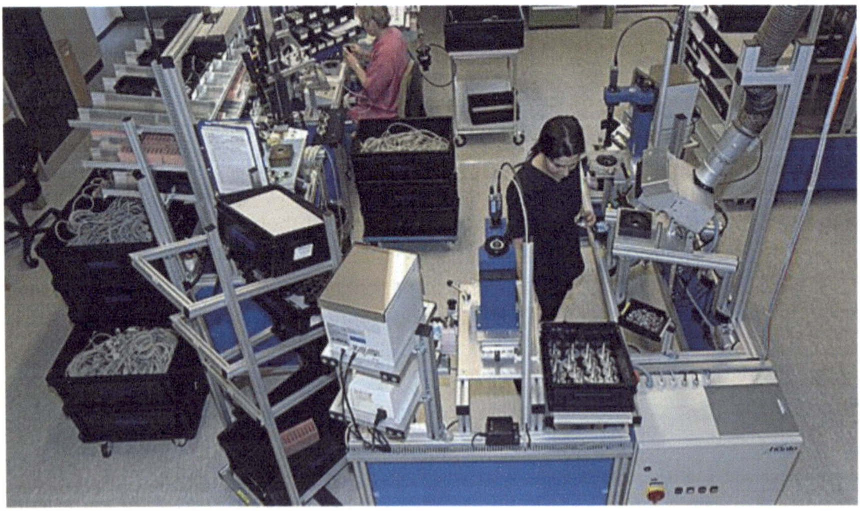

Fig. 7.4 Chaku Chaku line. (Source: Author's source)

through cars. We envision cars existing sustainably with the earth and society, and we will continue to tackle challenges with creative ideas".

1. Brighten people's lives through car ownership.
2. Offer cars that are sustainable with the earth and society to more people.
3. Embrace challenges and seek to master the Doh ("Way" or "Path") of creativity.

Mazda's Brand Essence is "Celebrate Driving". "Celebrate Driving" delivered by Mazda is not just about driving performance. The aim of the branding is: choosing a Mazda shall prize the customer and user with confidence and pride. Additionally, driving a Mazda is also leading up to urge to take on new challenges. Not just our products but every encounter with Mazda evokes the emotion of motion and makes customers' hearts beat with excitement. All of these are contained in our brand essence of "Celebrate Driving". This marketing strategy targets not only existing users but also new customers who are willing to change from existing brands (Mazda 2019). Mazda is a company with the headquarters in Hiroshima (Japan) and uses Toyota methods in operations across the factories and supply chain. Toyota is all about the process about eliminating waste. Mazda is using lean tools like 5S, Kanban cards, Andon, and poka-yoke. All of them are used to improve and optimize the processes through small changes (Kaizen). Mazda is all about making cars. Mazda's lean management starts with the design of each vehicle, in which engineers are brought together with experts from supply chain and manufacturing to make sure that the cars can be produced in the best and most ergonomic way as possible. Mazda states that a car is not simply a bunch of products and metal, but it's a living creature with emotional bound to its driver. That is Mazda's ultimate goal of Kodo, the "Soul of Motion" design.

There are ten plants in Toyota city and just one with two assembly lines in Hiroshima. Toyota has another 2 plants in Japan and 25 over the world. Mazda has one more plant in Japan plus five manufacturing and four assembly plants worldwide. As a result, in 2016 Toyota produced over ten million vehicles, where Mazda assembled over 1.5 million. With Toyota focus on process, there's no surprise their production system is made to be super effective. Cars were moving fast on the assembly line. Workers had precisely defined, simple tasks to perform within short cycle. Toyota's operators spend less than half a minute per station (cycle times). Everything was packed in a small area, so the distances between workstations were minimal.

On the other hand, everything in Mazda was just slower. The cycle times for each operation in Mazda are longer, and workers have more tasks to perform on single units. Mazda is using also lean tools such as Kanban, Andon, and poka-yoke. There is less automation in Mazda. As a result, Mazda assembly line takes significantly more space. In Mazda, it takes 15 hours from stamping to final inspection in Mazda and 17 hours in Toyota's Takaoka Plant (Fig. 7.5).

Fig. 7.5 Mazda headquarters, Hiroshima. (Source: Author's source)

References

Bertagnolli, F. (2018). *Lean management*. Wiesbaden: Springer.

Helmold, M., & Samara, W. (2019). *Progress in performance management. Industry insights and case studies on principles, application tools, and practice*. Heidelberg: Springer.

Helmold, M., Dathe, T., & Hummel, F. (2019). *Erfolgreiche Verhandlungen – Best-in-Class Empfehlungen für den Verhandlungsdurchbruch*. Wiesbaden: Springer.

James, R., Lincoln, M. L., Takahashi, G., & Takahashi, P. (1997). Keiretsu networks in the Japanese economy: An analysis of Intercorporate ties. *American Sociological Review., 57*(5), 561–585.

Mazda. (2019). www.mazda.com.

Wykowski, T. (2019). 3 Ways Mazda differs from Toyota. https://procognita.com/post/3-ways-mazda-differs-from-toyota-404/.

8 Lean Management in the Product Development

The most dangerous waste is the waste we do not recognize.

Shigeo Shingo (1909–1990)

8.1 Design for Lean Manufacturing

Design for lean manufacturing is the process in the product development phase, in which lean principles will be applied in the design and product development phase. The term describes methods of design in lean manufacturing companies as part of the product development and concept phase.

Lean design utilizes methods such as process simulations or modelling tools for achieving the optimal design of a product or process in the most efficient way. Preserving value with less work can be accomplished through "lean" methods of design and problem-solving.

Figure 8.1 shows the value chain with functions like bidding, product development, production, and after-sales. The lean vision including design for manufacturing will allocate resources to the development phase in order to have a robust product and production process. The term frontloading is associated with this concept and will prevent from fire fighting due to a better design.

Design for lean manufacturing is a process for applying lean concepts to the design phase of a system, such as a complex product or process. The term describes methods of design in lean manufacturing companies as part of the study of Japanese industry by the Massachusetts Institute of Technology. At the time of the study, the Japanese automakers were outperforming the American counterparts in speed, resources used in design, and design quality. Conventional mass production design focuses primarily on product functions and manufacturing costs; however, design for lean manufacturing systematically widens the design equation to include all factors that will determine a product's success across its entire value stream and life

M. Helmold, *Lean Management and Kaizen*, Management for Professionals,
https://doi.org/10.1007/978-3-030-46981-8_8

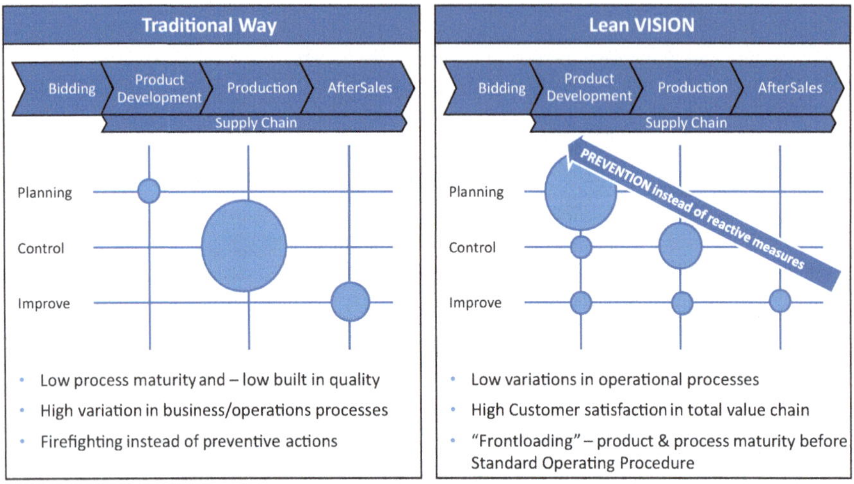

Fig. 8.1 Lean management in product development. (Source: Author's source)

cycle. One goal is to reduce waste and maximize value, and other goals include improving the quality of the design and reducing the time to achieve the final solution. The method has been used in architecture, healthcare, product development, processes design, and information technology systems and even to create lean business models. It relies on the definition and optimization of values coupled with the prevention of wastes before they enter the system. Design for lean manufacturing is system design.

8.2 Lean Management Concepts in Product Development

8.2.1 Case Study: Apple's Design Strategy

Lean is optimizing a process to preserve value with less work. Lean manufacturing is a management philosophy derived mostly from the Toyota Production System (TPS). Lean aims to eliminate waste in the entire value stream, by creating processes that need less human effort, less space, and less time to make products and services at lower cost; therefore, lean simply means creating more value for customers with fewer resources. However, how does this relate to Steve Jobs and iPod in particular or all Apple's iDevices in general? Steve Jobs used lean in another way; instead of thinking of lean as a way of minimizing waste in the production process, he looked at how to eliminate waste in the way the customer interacts with the iPod. For example, the volume up button could have different functions such as selecting a menu choice or taking a photo. This approach enabled Apple to produce mobile phones with just five buttons. Apple's (or perhaps Steve Jobs') innovation is by focusing on customers and how to offer them products without the unnecessary extras from design stage until displayed in an outlet.

There is a fine line between valuing the lessons demonstrated by great leaders and slipping into a blind devotion that masks the inevitable flaws to be found in every human personality. Steve Jobs had more than his share of flaws, and he possessed more than his share of genius. Reading Walter Isaacson's recent and excellent biography of Jobs, I am struck by the intuitive sense of lean, of flow, and of simplicity that he demanded from both the aesthetics and the technical workings of every product. You would be hard-pressed to find an executive with a better sense of the interaction between the social and the technical. When we think of lean, our mind first goes to the workings of the Toyota factory. However, the principles of eliminating waste and achieving interruption free flow may be found at an even more profound level in the design of Apple's breakthrough products and the intuition of Steve Jobs. Only 9 percent of Americans today work in manufacturing, and we might do well to turn our attention to the application of lean principles to less obvious endeavours such as product design and the use of technology. From the design of the first Mac to the design of the iPad, Steve obsessed on their design. He understood what we wanted before we wanted it and that was his genius. We didn't know we wanted GUIs, an iPod, or iPad and even less did we think we would be attracted to a product by the elegance and simplicity of its packaging. He imagined the customer experience before we had experienced it. This is intuition, a Zen appreciation for the movement of the hand and eye and the imperative to eliminate distractions to allow the mind of the user to flow from the first thought to the engagement in the utility of the device. As usual Jobs pushed for the purest simplicity. That required determining what was the core essence of the device. The answer: the display screen. So the guiding principle was that everything they did had to defer to the screen. "How do we get out of the way so there aren't a ton of features and buttons that distract from the display?" With the story of the development of each product, it is easy to see why Jobs nearly drove those around him crazy. It was normal for him to walk around and look at the work of designers and engineers and immediately pronounce their work to be crap! And, a week later he would be gushing about the very same thing he labelled "crap" a week earlier. It was also normal that the work on the new product would be almost finalized, or finalized in the mind of others, and he would wake up in the middle of the night and realize why he was not comfortable with its design. The radius of the corners was wrong! Or, the ionized aluminium casing wasn't exactly right. He would stop everything and have the entire team working on the product go back and fix things based on his simple feel for the design. Inevitably he would be proven right. And in every case, it was a matter of the flow, the movement of the eye and mind from one interaction with the product to the next. It was about "lean" although he would not have felt the need to label it as such. It wasn't the lean of the factory, but the lean of the customer experience. It is doubtable that any CEO in the history of business has been as intimately involved in the design of breakthrough products. His contribution was not that of a traditional executive at all. It was total intimacy with the customer experience that was his contribution. The way lean is implemented in many companies today it is viewed as primarily a cost reduction tool. Eliminating work in process, reducing the need for space, and increasing output per employee are all the natural results of lean, and all result in positive impact to the bottom line. Rarely was reducing costs the primary motivation behind Steve Jobs' decisions. The decision to open retail stores provides a telling example. Jobs obsessively wanted to control the entire flow of work from the design of chips to software to the design of the case, the screen, and the packing. This was the motivation for his decision to open Apple Stores. He and Ron Johnson spent many months designing the stores, developing prototypes, and obsessing on every detail. From a traditional retailing perspective, it made no sense. They didn't have enough different products to fill a store. Most analysts thought it would be impossible to push enough products through the stores to justify the cost of the space. Gateway was failing miserably in their retail stores, and Dell was selling direct to customers. But that is not how Jobs was thinking at all. He was thinking about the brand, the customer experience, and the joy that the stores would create. Larry Ellison, the CEO of Oracle, was a close friend, and Steve repeatedly invited him over to walk through his prototype store. On each visit Jobs prodded Ellison to figure out ways to streamline the process by eliminating some unnecessary step, such as handing over the credit card or printing a receipt. "If you look at the stores and the products, you will see Steve's obsession with beauty and simplicity – this Bauhaus aesthetic and wonderful minimalism, which goes all the way to the checkout process in the stores", said Ellison. "It means absolute minimum number of steps. Steve gave us the exact explicit recipe for how he wanted the checkout to work. That is lean thinking at its best".

Most experts predicted failure. "Maybe it's time Steve Jobs stopped thinking quite so differently". *Businessweek* wrote in a story headlines "Sorry Steve, Here's Why Apple Stores Won't Work". The retail consultant David Goldstein declared, "I give them two years before they're turning out the lights on a very painful and expensive mistake". Gateway's stores were averaging 250 visitors per week. On May 19, 2001, the first Apple Store opened in Tysons Corner Mall, one of the most expensive retail properties in the country. By 2004 Apple stores were averaging 5400 visitors per week! That year they had $1.2 billion in revenue, setting a record in the retail industry. In July 2011, a decade after the first store was opened, there were 326 Apple stores. The average annual revenue was $34 million, and the net sales in 2010 were $9.8 billion. They were not only profitable, but they boosted the brand and reinforced everything else that Apple did. The development of Apple stores and Apple products demonstrated an aspect of lean thinking that is not understood by most lean practitioners. It is not simply about cutting costs. It is about creating value in the customer experience by optimizing flow. Many lean writers and practitioners have not been willing to step up to the plate and address the issues of organizational structure and systems. But, if you don't you are not likely to be lean. The story of Sony's lost opportunity and the development of the iPod proves the point. Sony had a music division and contracts with a large number of the most popular bands and artists. They were a dominant force in the music business. They had another division that had created the Walkman, a personal device to carry and play music. They had a computer division producing personal computers. They even had software to sell music online. And, at the time, they realized that Napster and other free music download websites were destroying the profitability of their business. It was out of control. Within the Sony brand, they had every piece required to solve the problem. However, the three big and powerful divisions fought among themselves and could not collaborate to develop a solution. At Apple Computer there was a leader who understood disruptive technology. It wouldn't be unfair to call Steve Jobs the Crown Prince of disruptive technologies. At that time Apple was merely a personal computer company (Edson 2012). They produced no personal or portable devices. But, Jobs loved music. He understood that the personal computer could be the music hub. He personally led the charge to develop the iPod, and there were no warring divisions within Apple. Jobs personally met with music royalty including Bob Dylan, Bono, the head of Universal, Sony, and other music studios. He went to Japan and found the disc drive at Toshiba that could hold a thousand tunes. He developed an end-to-end solution that met the needs of the artists, the music studios, his own company, and, most importantly, the customers who loved music! He practically lived with Jony Ive, the chief designer, whose aesthetic sense of elegant simplicity for not only the device but even the packaging created a unique brand image and advantage. The combination of iTunes software for your computer, the iTunes store, and the iPod, met the needs of all key stakeholders. It was a victory of seamless integration. It eliminated waste in every component of the music delivery process. It could only have been achieved by an organization devoid of silos and a leader who understood the advantage of a seamless experience by the end user. In every instance of product development and marketing, Steve Jobs understood and demonstrated how eliminating waste from the flow of work and the flow of the customer experience results in the creation of value. Perhaps more than any other executive in our lifetime, he understood the interdependence of the human and technical factors in product development and in their use. This is the lean that needs more of our attention (Miller 2014).

References

Edson, J. (2012). *Design like apple: Seven principles for creating insanely great products, services, and experiences.* Hoboken, New Jersey: Canada.

Miller, L. (2014). Lean design – learning from apple. February 26, 2014 by BPIR.com Limited. Retrieved 22 Dec 2019. https://blog.bpir.com/customer-services/lean-design-learning-from-apple/.

Principles of a Lean Production System 9

All we are doing is looking at the time line, from the moment the customer gives us an order to the point when we collect the cash.

Taiichi Ohno (1912–1990)

9.1 Principles of a Lean Production System

9.1.1 Introduction

The just-in-time production system or lean production system can be described as the ideal combination of four principles (Imai 1986). These principles are the (1) zero-defect principle, (2) the pull principle, (3) the tact and the (4) flow principle as displayed in Fig. 9.1 (Helmold and Samara 2019).

9.1.2 Zero-Defect Principle

The starting point in Toyota's success story, zero defects is all about identifying errors or defects as closely as possible to where they occur. By so doing, and by neither accepting nor passing on defects, issues are resolved quickly and efficiently, avoiding subsequent rework and quality issues. The zero-defect principle is a concept of the Toyota Production System and is aimed at the reduction of defects through error prevention (Ohno 1990). It is directed at motivating people to prevent mistakes by developing a constant, conscious desire to do their job right the first time. In reality, zero defects are not possible; however, the concept ensures that there is no waste existing in a project (Helmold and Terry 2016). Waste refers to all unproductive processes, tools, employees, and so on. Anything that is unproductive

M. Helmold, *Lean Management and Kaizen*, Management for Professionals,
https://doi.org/10.1007/978-3-030-46981-8_9

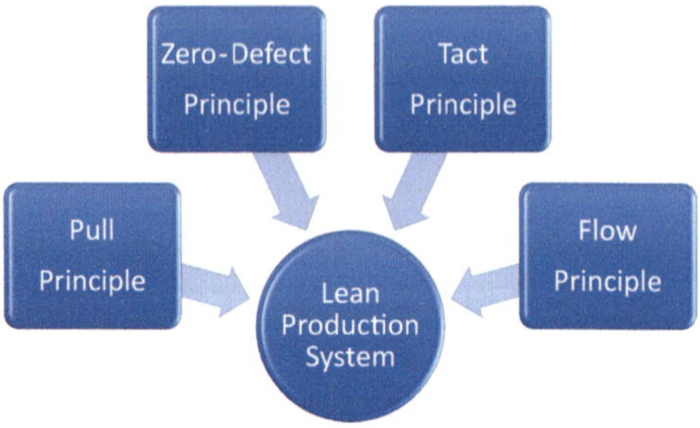

Fig. 9.1 Four lean production principles

and does not add value to a project should be eliminated, called the process of elimination of waste. Eliminating waste creates a process of improvement and correspondingly lowers costs. Common with the zero defects theory is the concept of "doing it right the first time" to avoid costly and time-consuming fixes later in the project management process. The concept of zero defects is grounded on four major elements for implementation in real projects:

- Quality is a state of assurance to requirements. Therefore, zero defects in a project means fulfilling requirements at that point in time.
- Right the first time. Quality should be integrated into the process from the beginning, rather than solving problems at a later stage.
- Quality is measured in financial terms. One needs to judge waste, production, and revenue in terms of budgetary impact.
- Performance should be judged by the accepted standards, as close to perfection as possible.

9.1.3 Pull Principle

The pull system is one of the lean manufacturing principles and is used to reduce waste in the production process. In this type of system, components used in the manufacturing process are only replaced once they have been consumed, so companies only make enough products to meet customer demand. The opposite principle is the push system, in which as many products as possible are generated to be sold via marketing activities. The principles aim to avoid overproduction and stockpiling, thereby saving working capital, by letting demand dictate the rate at which goods or services are delivered. In this way the customer, or the next step in the chain, "pulls" value through the process.

9.1.4 Flow Principle

Value should be added in a smooth, uninterrupted flow, from the start to the end of the production process. The ultimate effect of this principle is that all process steps

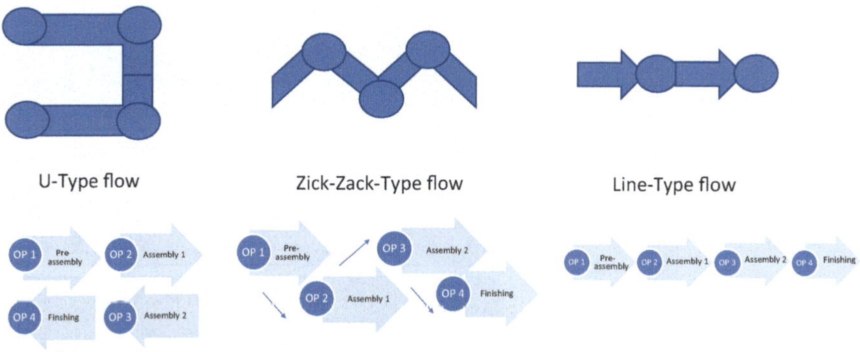

Fig. 9.2 Types of flows in operations. (Source: Marc Helmold)

are focused and aligned to adding value, one piece at a time, removing all wasteful and unnecessary activities from the process. The advantage of a continuous flow in operations is that it features stability, continuity and balance and doesn't waste time (the nonrenewable resource). No time wasted on waiting between steps means time is being maximized for its capabilities. Operations are not able to introduce a wasteless process without the continuous flow, as it is the truly ideal process state. However, the troubles with continuous flow are that it's very hard to achieve, process steps aren't generally balanced, and all process contains inherent waste activities. When one starts out to achieve continuous flow, many process problems will appear and come to the surface. Most individuals think this is bad – it's actually a good thing. The optimal process features continuous flow, and any problems that stand in your way from achieving continuous flow are problems that are now visible and can be rectified. The ideal flow is the one-piece flow as shown in Fig. 9.2.

9.1.5 Tact Principle

The German word for timing, tact, refers to the rhythm at which goods or services are produced to meet customer demand. With a consistent, continuous rhythm providing a heartbeat for your production processes, it is far easier to regulate, responding flexibly and effortlessly as demand rises or falls. Tact time is defined as the average time available (time available minus breaks, maintenance or setup) divided by the customer requested quantity as shown in Fig. 9.3.

The average time between the start of production of one unit and the start of production of the next unit, when these production starts, is set to match the rate of customer demand. For example, if a customer wants 15 units with the available time of 9 minutes and the steady flow through the production line, the average time between production starts should be 36 seconds for one part or unit (9 minutes multiplied by 60 seconds = 540 seconds; 540 seconds divided by 15 unites requested by the customer = 36 seconds per part). In fact, the tact time simply reflects the rate of production needed to match the demand. In the previous example, whether it takes

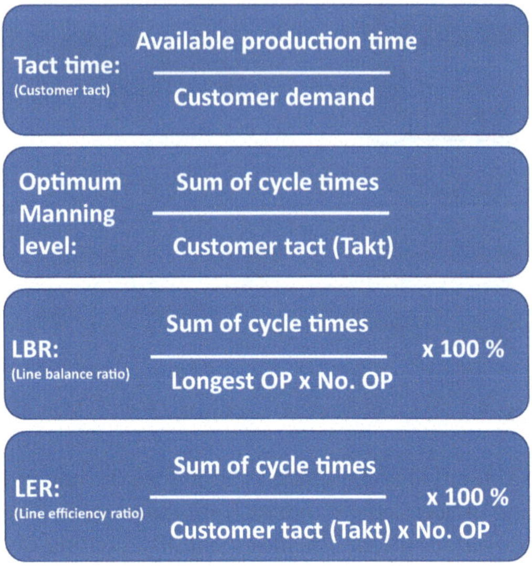

Fig. 9.3 Tact time and other ratios

4 minutes or 4 years to produce the product, the tact time is based on customer demand. If a process or a production line is unable to produce at tact time, either demand levelling, additional resources, or process reengineering is needed to correct the issue (Helmold and Terry 2016).

- Directly tie production efficiencies to fiscal reporting.
- Reduce investigation time for root cause analysis.
- Shorten equipment ROI through increased utilization.
- Decrease costs through waste elimination.
- Increase customer satisfaction through quality improvement.

9.2 Andon

Andon (Japanese: アンドン or あんどん or 行灯) is a lean manufacturing tool referring to a system to notify management, maintenance, and other workers of a quality or process problem. The centrepiece is a device incorporating signal lights to indicate which workstation has the problem. The alert can be activated manually by a worker using a pull cord or button, or may be activated automatically by the production equipment itself. The system may include a means to stop production so the issue can be corrected. Some modern alert systems incorporate audio alarms, text, or other displays. An Andon system is one of the principal elements of the Jidoka method pioneered by Toyota as part of the TPS and therefore now part of the lean concept. It gives the worker the ability, and moreover the empowerment, to stop production when a defect is found and immediately calls for assistance. Common reasons for manual activation of the Andon are part shortage, defect created or found, tool malfunction, or the existence of a safety problem. Work is stopped until

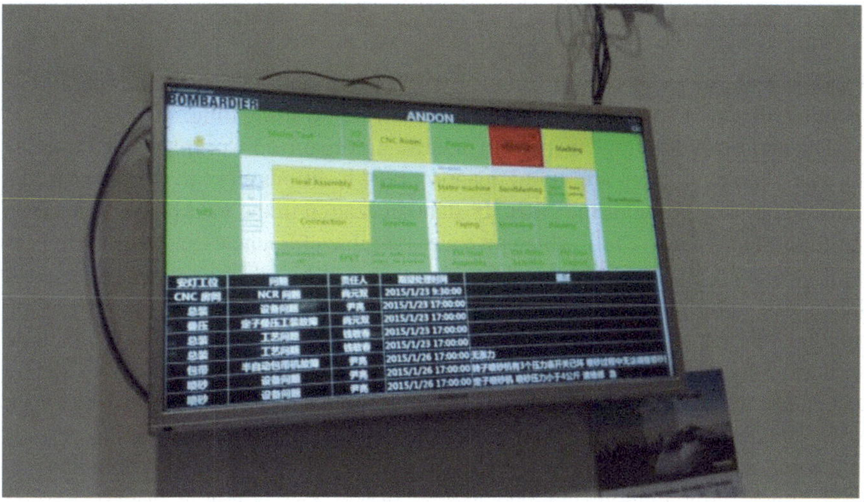

Fig. 9.4 Andon

a solution has been found. The alerts may be logged to a database so that they can be studied as part of a continuous improvement program. The system typically indicates where the alert was generated and may also provide a description of the trouble. Modern Andon systems can include text, graphics, or audio elements. Audio alerts may be done with coded tones, music with different tunes corresponding to the various alerts, or pre-recorded verbal messages. Usage of the word originated within Japanese manufacturing companies and in English is a loanword from a Japanese word for a paper lantern (Imai 1986) (Fig. 9.4).

9.3 Poka-Yoke

Poka-yoke (ポカヨケ) is a Japanese term that means "mistake-proofing". A poka-yoke is any mechanism in a lean concept process that helps an equipment operator avoid (*yokeru*) mistakes (*poka*). Its purpose is to eliminate product defects by preventing, correcting, or drawing attention to human or other errors as they occur. The concept was formalized, and the term adopted, by Shigeo Shingo as part of the TPS. It was originally described as baka-*yoke*, but as this means "fool-proofing" (or "idiot-proofing"), the name was changed to the milder *poka-yoke*.

9.4 Gemba and Shopfloor

Gemba (現場 also described as *gemba*) is also a Japanese term meaning the real or right place. A production environment considers the shopfloor as the most important place and the employees in the operation and support functions as most important human capital for adding value.

9.5 Shadow Boards

Shadow boards are specific boards for parts, tools, and equipment in operations, manufacturing, or service areas to reduce waste and waiting time.

The aim of the shadow board is to achieve an organized workplace where tools, supplies, and equipment are stored in appropriate locations close to the work area or work stations. It provides the basis for standardization in the workplace. They are a simple and inexpensive tool which provides tangible efficiencies and cost savings as well as intangible benefits. Figure 9.5 shows a shadow board for screws in Mitsubishi Japan. The appropriate storage, allocation, and preparation of screws avoid waiting time and the possibility of errors. The advantages of using shadow boards include avoiding waste, such as time looking for the appropriate tool or even having to buy a new one and wasted time in looking for supplies and interchanging tools between tasks. Shadow boards also provide the ability to quickly gauge the location of tools and equipment or if they are missing. Shadow boards are used in the sort and set in order stages of the implementation and operation of a 5S system in a workplace and kaizen initiatives. Shadow boards can be different sizes and located in many different areas of a process or plant. The key is that they are appropriately located and hold all the necessary tools for the area or workstation (Fig. 9.5).

9.6 Health and Safety

Health, safety, and environment (HSE) is the concept and paradigm that implements and secures practical aspects of environmental protection and safety at work. From a health and safety standpoint, it involves creating organized efforts and procedures for identifying workplace hazards and reducing accidents and exposure to harmful situations and substances. It also includes training of personnel in accident prevention, accident response, emergency preparedness, and use of protective clothing and equipment. From an environmental standpoint, it involves creating a systematic approach to complying with environmental regulations, such as managing waste or air emissions all the way to helping operations´ departments reduce the company's carbon footprint. Successful HSE programs also include measures to address ergonomics, air quality, and other aspects of workplace safety that could affect the health and well-being of employees and the overall community. Figure 9.6 displays HSE requirements in a Chinese operations environment.

9.7 Overall Equipment Effectiveness (OEE)

Manufacturing a product is a complex process. Without clear and numerical objectives and guidelines, it is very easy to lose control in the production process. OEE is a tool that combines multiple manufacturing issues and data points to provide information about the process. By analysing and calculating data, it also functions as a framework for root cause analysis. Through a documented process of combining the

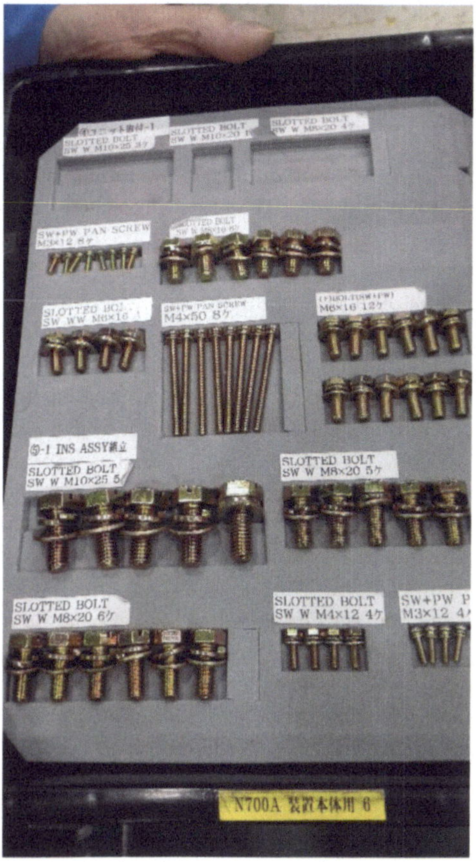

Fig. 9.5 Shadow board. (Source: Helmold. Shadow board. Mitsubishi Shinkanzen production in Osaka)

underlying data, OEE provides specific process information. All members of the manufacturing team, from assembly technicians to financial personnel, can use the data to understand the current state of the manufacturing process. By having a predetermined framework of the impact of machine availability, performance, and quality, OEE provides a framework to track underlying issues and root causes. OEE also provides a framework for improvements in the manufacturing process. By using key OEE concepts such as The Six Big Losses, waste exposed by tracking OEE can be understood and efficiencies can be improved. The components of this framework are:

- Availability
- Performance
- Quality

OEE is a very simple metric to immediately indicate the current status of a manufacturing process and also a complex tool allowing you to understand the effect of the various issues in the manufacturing process and how they affect the entire process (OEE = Availability x Performance x Quality). Availability refers to the machine or cell being available for production when scheduled. At the most basic level, when a process is running, it is creating value for the end user. When a process is stopped, it's creating a cost with no associated value. Whether it's due to mechanical failure, raw materials, or operator issues, the cell or machine is either producing or not producing. By comparing scheduled run time to actual run time, the availability component of OEE allows for a determination of lost production due to downtime. Performance is determined by how much waste is created through running at less than optimal speed. By comparing the actual cycle times against ideal cycle times, OEE allows for a determination of how much production was lost by cycles that did not meet the ideal cycle time. Quality focuses on identifying time that was wasted by producing a product that does not meet quality standards. By comparing the quantity of good to reject parts, the percent of time actually adding value by producing good product is exposed. By itself, OEE only provides data about your manufacturing process. Companies that use OEE as a metric have found success when combining it with general lean manufacturing programs and also as part of TPM systems. When using OEE with these systems, the benefits become significant: Fig. 9.6 shows an example of the OEE. High-performing companies can achieve an OEE higher than 85 percent. (Helmold and Samara 2019). In the calculation, the OEE has the elements availability (83.3%), performance (90.0%), and quality (98%). Based on the actual figures, it is now possible to optimize each at the inefficient categories. The availability ratio is below 90% and needs special actions for improvements (Fig. 9.7).

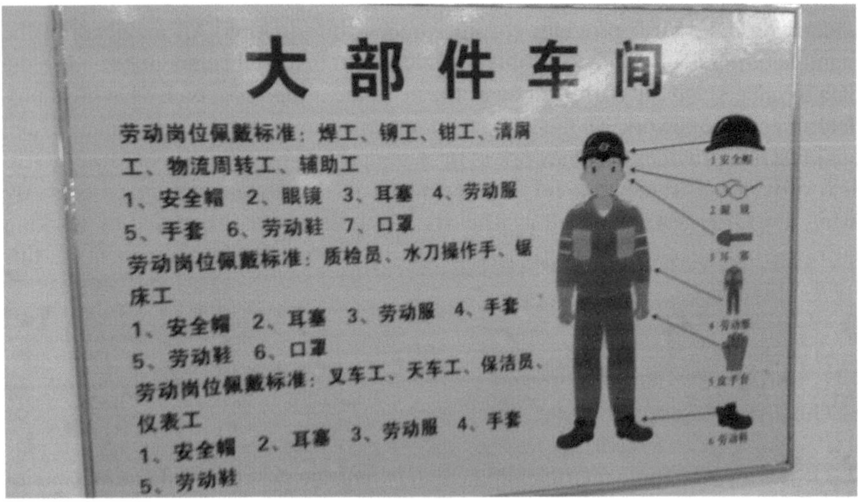

Fig. 9.6 Health, safety, and environment. (Source: Author's source)

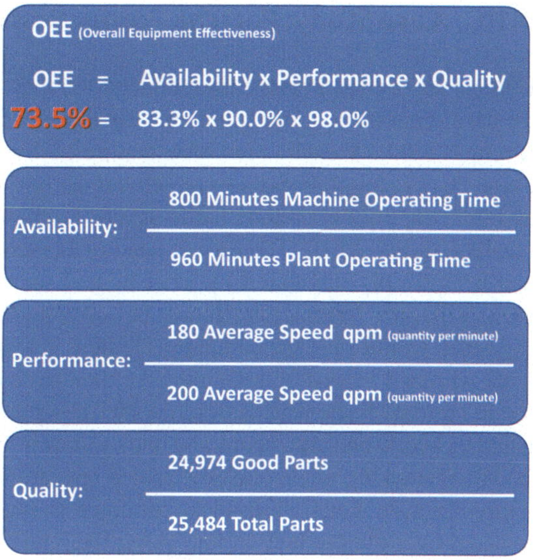

Fig. 9.7 OEE calculation. (Source: Author's source)

9.8 Kanban

Kanban (看板) is a visual system for managing work as it moves through a process. It is a concept related to lean and just-in-time (JIT) production, where it is used as a scheduling system that tells you what to produce, when to produce it, and how much to produce. Initially it arose as a scheduling system for lean manufacturing, originating from the Toyota Production System (TPS).

9.9 Supermarkets

Supermarkets ordinarily are located near the supplying process to help that process see customer usage and requirements. Each item in a supermarket has a specific location from which a material handler withdraws products in the precise amounts needed by a downstream process. As an item is removed, a signal to make more (such as a Kanban card or an empty bin) is taken by the material handler to the supplying process. Toyota installed its first supermarket in 1953 in the machine shop of its main plant in Toyota City (Ohno 1990). Toyota executive Taiichi Ohno took the idea for the supermarket from photos of American supermarkets showing goods arrayed on shelves by specific location for withdrawal by customers.

9.10 Case Study: Porsche Production System

Companies such as Porsche have understood that the low value-adding activities of the own organization lead automatically to increasing activities on the supply side (Freitag 2004). Porsche was also hampered by antiquated production methods. Some 20 percent of its parts were delivered 3 or more days too late, for example. In addition, supply disruptions led to severe problems in the value chain and caused recalls (Greiml 2010). The former head of Porsche, Dr. Wendelin Wiedeking, who had been deeply impressed by what he had seen on visits to Japanese auto firms such as Toyota, Nissan, and Honda, believed that only a radical, "lean manufacturing" cure would save the company. He flew in teams of the same Japanese consultants who had helped Toyota and gave them free rein. "A cultural revolution from top to bottom" is the way he describes what happened next, as the consultants organized the workforce into teams and one by one eliminated poor practices (Kalkowsky 2004). Wiedeking made one now-fabled appearance on the assembly line wielding a circular saw, which he used to cut down the roof-high racks of spare parts that towered over the production line. After the lean cure of the own production facilities, Porsche extended the lean concept to suppliers and established the supplier development department in 2006 (the name of the department is FEL, Finance-Purchasing, Supply Management). This department is in charge of extending lean principles to the supply networks and to synchronize production systems. In the following section, the concept of lean supply management will be discussed. Lean principles have:

- To apply lean principles throughout the supply chain
- To integrate suppliers
- To be customer oriented
- To have flat hierarchies
- To establish competencies to core functions
- To apply lean principles to shopfloor (gemba)
- To concentrate only on essential success factors
- To reduce waste
- To continuously improve
- To apply a pull system
- To apply a learning organization

References

Freitag, M. (2004). Toyota. Formel Toyota. *Manager Magzin, 12*, 12–14.

Greiml, H. (2010). The Toyota recall crisis. Toyota recalls 1.1m vehicles to fix floor mats. *Automotive News*, 12–15.

Helmold, M., & Samara, W. (2019). *Progress in performance management. Industry insights and case studies on principles, application tools, and practice*. Heidelberg: Springer.

Helmold, M., & Terry, B. (2016). *Global sourcing and supply management excellence in China. Procurement guide for supply experts*. Singapore: Springer.

Imai, M. (1986). *Kaizen. Der Schlüssel zum Erfolg der Japaner im Wettbewerb*. Frankfurt: Ullstein.

Kalkowsky, M. (2004). Nur Porsche hat das lean management begriffen: Interview with prof. D. Jones. *PRO, 31*, 16.

Ohno, T. (1990). *Toyota Production System. Beyond large Scale Production*. New York: Productivity Press.

Lean Management on the Upstream (Supply Side) 10

What gets measured gets improved.

Peter Drucker (1909–2005)

10.1 Supply Side

The term supply management as key value-adding function replaces old definitions of procurement or purchasing. This definition is in line with Porter's description of value chains (Porter 1985). A value chain is a set of activities that a firm operating in a specific industry performs in order to deliver a valuable product, service for the market (Kuerble et al. 2016). The concept comes from business management and was first described and popularized by Michael E. Porter in his 1985 best seller, *Competitive Advantage: Creating and Sustaining Superior Performance*, in the upstream supply management or the supply side. Figure 10.1 displays the operations, the upstream supply side (supply management), and the downstream supply side (customer or demand side side). In Porter's value chain framework (see Fig. 10.2), inbound logistics, operations, outbound logistics, marketing and sales, and service are categorized as primary activities. Secondary activities include procurement, human resource management, technological development, and infrastructure. As many companies have external value chains (purchase of goods, services) of more than 80 percent, supply management has here the most significant role in any enterprise. In many enterprises, functions are still working independently from each other, leading to a large amount of waste and inefficiencies. Many industries are currently faced by fierce competition. This is forcing manufacturing companies to concentrate on core competencies and to transfer the production of components, goods, and services to external suppliers (Aberdeen Group 2005, 2006). The number of value-adding activities has decreased constantly and now lies between

M. Helmold, *Lean Management and Kaizen*, Management for Professionals,
https://doi.org/10.1007/978-3-030-46981-8_10

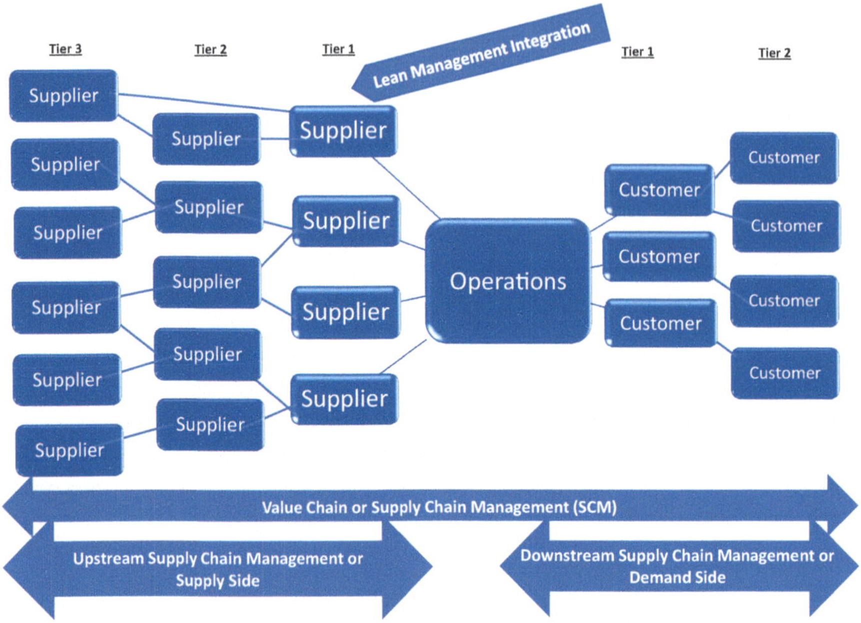

Fig. 10.1 Lean integration in the upstream supply chain or supply side

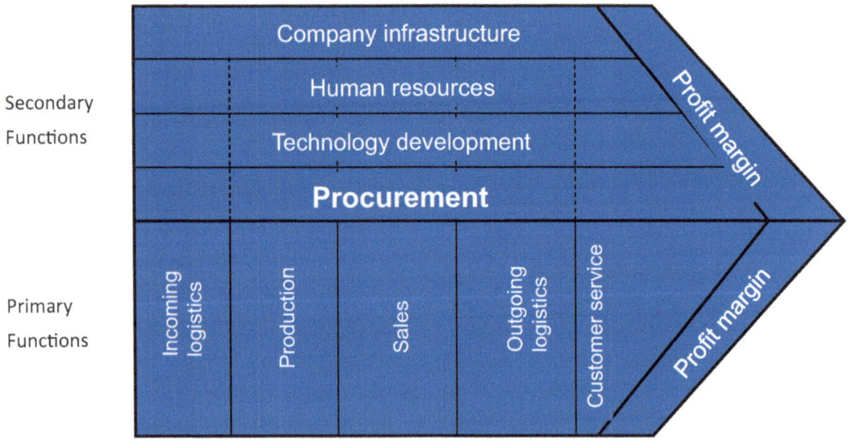

Fig. 10.2 Porter's value chain. (Source: Author's source, adopted from Helmold et al. (2020))

10 and 30 percent in this industry (Dyer 1996). The company Apple has no production and decided to outsource the manufacturing of iPads or iPhones to the company Foxconn. Such a development has had a great influence on the structure of supply chains and supplier relationships. Supply chains (the terms "supply chains" and "supply networks" are used synonymously in the literature)

have become more complex and international; as pointed out by several authors, Christopher and Peck see the level of complexity increasing in the upstream supply chain management of manufacturing companies in many industries, a trend which is characterized by the growing transfer of activities to suppliers and supplier networks, high numbers of supply chain layers (tiers), and the ongoing globalization of supply chains (Christopher and Peck 2004). As a consequence, vulnerability and risk exposure have risen significantly. The rapid increase in supplier activities therefore directly affects supply management, as emphasized by Emmett and Crocker (2009). In recent years, many companies have reduced their value-adding activities and implemented efficiency-oriented cost reductions, e.g. outsourcing, single sourcing, low-cost country sourcing, platform concepts, lean management, and design-to-cost approaches (Aberdeen group 2005; Gürtler and Spinler 2010). Supply management has become more important in core and peripheral business areas (Trkman and McCormack 2009) and is aimed at building resilient supply chains (Christopher and Peck 2004). Resilience is based on being able to anticipate, manage, and prevent supply chain disruptions at an early stage (Christopher and Peck 2004). On the other hand, supply risks have risen due to increased dependency on supplier networks.

In their research "An Empirical Analysis of the Effect of Supply Chain Disruptions on Long-Run Stock Price", found that enterprises without operational slack and redundancies in their supply chains experience negative stock effects. The authors revealed the tremendous impact of supply chain disruptions on stock price performance and shareholder value. Supply disruptions can easily lead to high recovery cost, waste, and sharp decreases in sales. External customers become dissatisfied, and internal core functions (e.g. assembly) are disturbed. In most cases, supply disruptions have negative impacts on brand image, sales figures, and the company's own financial situation as stressed by many authors writing about supply disruptions and resilient supply chains (Trkman and McCormack 2009). Recent incidents in the media about disruptions caused by upstream supply management inefficiencies from China show that the supply management excellence approach needs to tackle these issues in a proactive and sustainable way.

Supply management risks have mainly been investigated at the direct level of tier one relationships, but consideration has not been fully extended to sub-suppliers, i.e. tiers one, two, three, and beyond. The new concept of supply management therefore seeks to address these concerns by investigating how disruptions can be anticipated, prevented, and managed over the entire value chain including all tiers on the supply and demand side as shown in the figure by Slack et al. (1995). Recent supply disruptions show that current supply management organizations, tools, and concepts are not smart and resilient enough to avoid these supply chain discrepancies. Recent articles, for example, in the magazine *Automotive News*, show that all car producers are facing severe problems due to suppliers' problems. Not only the automotive industry but also many other industries face these issues.

The lean supply management concept was developed by Ohno (1990), who worked for Toyota Motors. It derived from a bundle of instruments which come from sophisticated production methods or supporting functions such as logistics. The ideal interplay and optimal combination of all instruments are essential for success. The vision of lean production is based on the *just-in-time* (JIT) philosophy and the Toyota Production System (TPS: Japanese = トヨタ生産システム) and focuses on the elimination of waste and the minimization of stock.

10.2 Supply Management Objectives

Supply side objectives are important. The seven rights (7R), which are the major objectives according to the lean supply management philosophy, can be defined as:

1. Right products
2. Right quality
3. Right time
4. Right quantity
5. Right location
6. Right people
7. Right cost

The right product refers to the right specification and requirements by the demanding customer. The products must have the required dimensions, layout, material, colour, etc. The right quality means the clarification of all requirements in terms of quality and improvement measures to have the optimum quality levels. Quality is normally measured by hard factors such as non-conformities, field rejects, or defects at receipt (0 km defects). The right quantity is the placing of a specific order quantity triggered by internal and customer demands. Supply management has to transfer the customer and company demands to the supply networks. The right time means that products ordered have to be at the buyer's place in time, neither too early nor too late. Supply management has to recognize suppliers' lead times. The lead time for any product starts from the order until the physical receipt of goods at the ordering party. The right location can be defined as the place where the products are required. Shipment of products from China to Europe takes more than 8 weeks, so that that the right location is closely linked to the lead time of products. The meaning of right people extends current definition of the five rights in line with the modern and lean philosophy of the new paradigm of supply management. Suppliers in global markets need to have the right sales people, project managers, and operators to meet the requested criteria. Project managers must have sufficient language skills, and operators must be trained to produce good quality parts. People are becoming in a changing and global trade situation more and more important.

Any product needs to have the right cost level; otherwise it will not be demanded and bought.

10.3 Lean Thinking as Part of Lean Supply Management

10.3.1 Supply Management Process

Industries or companies which have outsourced a large scope of their products to global supply networks would especially benefit from such research in supply management, supplier relationship management, and supply networks. In conclusion, it is evident that proactive supply management requires a subset of principles (see Fig. 10.3): The principles can be described as follows:

1. Supply management is a function which is managing the entire value chain; therefore supply management must be incorporated into the mission, values, and strategies of every organization.
2. Supply management best practices are focused on a multilayer approach, involving not only tier one but also tier two and three levels; proactive supply management can only be introduced and executed if the corporate objectives are communicated and cascaded throughout the organization; the setup must be centralized as single point of contact to suppliers.
3. Advanced and innovative supply management has standardized tools and processes.
4. Supply management best practice companies have sophisticated B2B platforms/supplier portals in terms of quality, cost, and delivery and other suitable KPIs.
5. Supply management and mitigation action activities have to be preventive, proactive, and sustainable; activities have to be oriented long term.

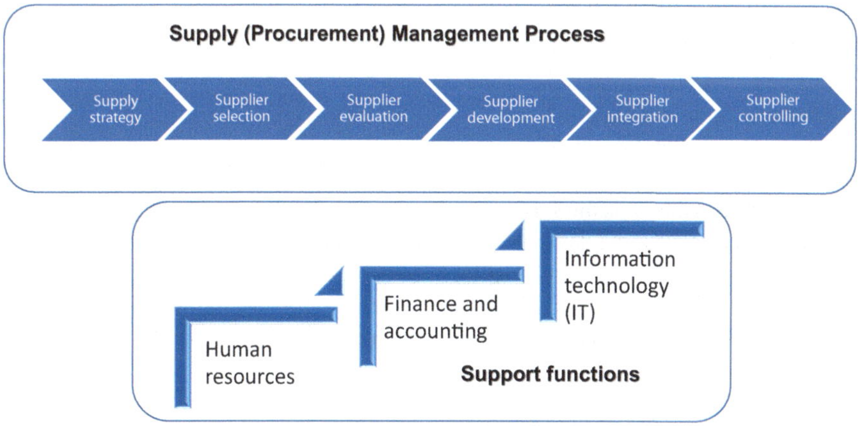

Fig. 10.3 Supply management process. (Source: Author's source)

6. Supply management requires a collaborative approach, including strategic alliances with suppliers. Such activities should be organized centrally.
7. Proactive supply management can be performed with a key account manager in terms of being a single point of contact for the supplier (customer).
8. Performance indicators have to be mutually agreed upon and may comprise both hard and soft factors. The assessment process should consist of quality, cost, delivery, and technological criteria.
9. The learning organization should, among other things, be characterized by the capability and competencies of coaching suppliers.
10. All the abovementioned principles should be combined with a philosophy of continuous improvement (Japanese: kaizen) and reflection (Japanese: hansei) to achieve a best practice model in supply management.

Companies that want to distance themselves from their competitors through best-in-class supply management must implement the ten principles and adopt a collaborative approach in dealing with their supply base. Appropriate management of one's supply base can lead to competitive advantage. The strategic objective of supply management is the establishment, design, and management of supplier networks and the successful collaboration within these networks as the figure shows. The network consists of internal and external suppliers. The collaboration between supply partners and the management of the interactions are a key responsibility of the supply management function. A sophisticated information system is a prerequisite for proper interactions.

10.3.2 Supply Management Strategy

Strategic supplier and materials segmentation (portfolio analysis).

Strategic supplier and commodity strategies are a suitable tool in supply management to secure supply of standard, leverage, shortage, and strategic materials (Hofbauer et al. 2012).

- Strategic suppliers/materials
- Leverage suppliers/materials
- Shortage suppliers/materials
- Standard suppliers/materials

Strategic Materials/Components

Strategic materials can be defined as special materials which are important and key to the own production of an enterprise. Siemens and Bombardier Transportation produce car bodies by themselves; however, aluminium and stainless steel or steel profiles and extrusions are strategic for the production and quality of the end product.

Leverage Materials/Components
Leverage materials can be defined where the supply side is characterized by many companies which offer the materials. The automotive industry is characterized by more than 10 to 20 different suppliers, which deliver entertainment products (polipolistic market).

Shortage Materials/Components
Shortage materials can be defined as materials that are scarce on the market. Scarcity represents a problem to any supply management organization and needs the right establishment of strategies.

Standard or Catalogue Materials/Components
Standard materials are materials that can be bought on the market. Often standard goods are catalogue products like screws, C-parts, etc.

10.3.3 Supply Management Selection and Evaluation

Supplier evaluation is the systematic assessment of existing or new suppliers on the basis of certain categories (Fig. 10.4). A supplier evaluation must be:

- A preventive and proactive system
- A KPI-based methodology

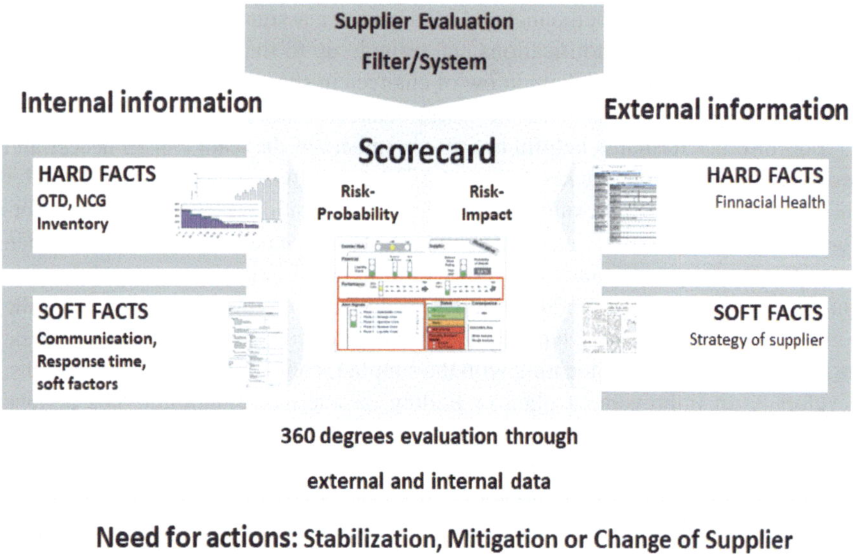

Fig. 10.4 Supplier evaluation

- An anticipating (sensoric) model
- A holistic and cross-functional assessment
- A standardized process
- An integrated supply base approach

These categories can be performance of the delivery, price evolution, production capacity, quality of management, technical capabilities, and service. Once there is a mechanism in place to periodically collect performance data from suppliers, the next step is to review the performance data. Ideally, the format that the data is in should lend itself to comparison and analysis. The data should also be in a format that can be quantified and scored. Many companies use a supplier evaluation or scorecard for this. Moreover, data from different types of assessments such as internal surveys, external surveys, and site visits should be incorporated into the analysis. Since most large organizations have many strategic suppliers and lots of data, it is almost impossible to obtain, organize, and review data from assessments effectively on a large scale without automation or software. When evaluating supplier performance data, the two things to look for (besides the obvious) are large changes in the performance metrics and overall trends. By identifying trends, a company can make projections about where the performance data will be in the future and can take action accordingly. Downward trends and deterioration in performance can signal a problem. Moreover, an abrupt change in performance metrics might signal an imminent problem. However, there could be another explanation. In this case it makes sense to obtain more data from the supplier and to dig deeper to find the source of the problem. It may be a one-time anomaly, or it could be something more. Monitoring supplier performance proactively can ensure that exceptions to policies are tracked and personnel and resources are assigned to address the problem quickly. Alerts and notifications can provide up to the minute information to company personnel letting them know of changes in supplier performance.

Having a system that can take the assessment/scorecard data and can output it in a report or other format is helpful because members of the team can all access and review the information quickly and easily. The performance evaluation of Daimler shown in Fig. 10.4 is an example of a supplier evaluation. For part C the performance is very bad, so that immediate actions have to be taken. Once there is sudden drop in supplier performance or a downward trend, it is important to take action quickly. Quick action can reduce the risk of disaster significant loss and gives the company the ability to take steps to prevent bad outcomes. Some actions that can be instigated include communicating with the supplier, conducting further evaluations, developing an improvement plan, or finding an alternative supplier. The actions taken may depend on many factors. These include the supplier's past performance, level of current performance, strategic importance, possible damages, and overall risk. One of the first things to do is to contact the supplier and find out what went wrong and why. The results of the performance assessment should be provided to the supplier and can create a basis for discussions.

The poor performance could have been the result of something outside of the supplier's control. It could have been a problem with process, personnel, a supplier, or something else. By communicating with the supplier, personnel can determine the cause of the problem and try to work with the supplier to make changes to bring the supplier performance back into compliance with the contract or with company policies. If the vendor does not have a good explanation or understanding of why the problem occurred, this may be a sign of trouble. Once the causes of a problem or set of problems have been identified, the next step is to devise a supplier improvement plan. The plan should be specific to the problem, should involve both company personnel and supplier personnel, and should involve a time line for addressing the problem or bringing the performance into compliance. This process should also be a collaborative process and should be aimed at improving the overall supply chain. Even if a supplier's performance is acceptable, the company may wish to invest time and resources in developing suppliers and improving suppler performance. If the problem is too severe, cannot be fixed in a timely manner, or poses too great of a risk, the company may wish to stop doing business altogether with the supplier. This means that the company should carefully find an alternative source of supply and, if possible, reduce its reliance on the supplier in question. Emmett and Crocker (2009) and Dust et al. (2010) also propose using such criteria for evaluating the performance of suppliers. Interestingly, the interviews revealed that many companies have created subcriteria of Q-C-D-SF according to their own needs. Regarding the question of how often manufacturing companies in the European transportation industry measure supplier performance, what they do internally with the data, and how they communicate the results to suppliers, several different answers were given. In the best case, data was updated on a weekly basis and made available to suppliers through a web-based tool. Concerning the evaluation of supplier performance, all interviewees outlined three to four categories, like traffic lights:

- Category one (green): acceptable with minor deviations and without conditions
- Category two (yellow): acceptable with conditions
- Category three (red): not acceptable

In category one (green), the evaluation is approved and accepted with minor deviations. In category two (yellow), the evaluation is accepted with conditions. Conditional acceptance means that any subsequent action plan has to be approved by the supply management department. If a supplier shows severe deficiencies and is categorized three (red), the evaluation is not accepted. This can mean that a new supplier is not allowed to supply parts. In cases where category three is measured during serial production, specific supply management actions (e.g. management escalation, supplier audits, dual-sourcing) might be the consequence. Some of the challenges associated with supplier evaluation may be mitigated by the use of appropriate tools. For simple projects, a spreadsheet can be used. But as evaluations become more complex or more frequent, data management and data integrity issues become significant. Web Electronic RFP/Tendering systems are often used for initial selection projects. Some products provide functionality for combining both initial selection and ongoing evaluation and benchmarking. Without few exceptions, there is no evaluation model which considers the maturity and level of relationship with suppliers (Helmold 2014). The doctoral thesis "Establishing a best practice model of supplier relationship management (SRM) for multinational manufacturing companies in the European transportation industry" makes suggestions for this aspect (Helmold 2014). There is also an MBA thesis available, which includes the assessment of the guanxi for supply management in China. Wider, within established supply management evaluation methodologies, the Carter 10 C's model is an internationally recognized approach. This model looks at aspects which should be evaluated before contracting and as part of the ongoing supplier performance appraisal. The ten categories can be summarized as the following:

1. Capacity (Does the organization have the capacity and capability to deliver the order?)
2. Competency (Is the organization, its people, or its process competent?)
3. Consistency (Does the organization produce a consistent output?)
4. Control of process (Can the organization control its process and offer flexibility?)
5. Commitment to quality (Does the organization effectively monitor and manage quality?)
6. Cash (Has the organization got a strong enough financial base?)
7. Cost (Is the product or service offered at a competitive price?)
8. Culture (Are the supplier and buyer cultures compatible?)
9. Clean (Is the organization ethical and funded legitimately and doesn't engage child labour?)
10. Communication efficiency (Does the organization have support technology of information integration?) to support collaboration and coordination in the supply chain

Fig. 10.5 Supplier dashboard

10.3.4 Control via Supplier Dashboard or Cockpit

A supply or supplier dashboard (or cockpit) provides management with an at-a-glance awareness of the status of certain performance indicators such as inventory and supply operations (see Fig. 10.5). Thus, it is possible to respond to challenges before any incident is happening. The supplier dashboard is showing key operational indicators and trends like NCG, OTD, outgoing quality, and sub-supplier performance. Indicators can vary from case to case.

A supplier dashboard or supplier cockpit is a one-page summary of the supplier's critical performance indicators as shown in the example above. The dashboard is supposed to give managers a quick overview of deteriorations and status on quality, delivery, or other critical issues. It enables the supply manager to take immediate actions based on a graphs or a colouring.

10.3.5 Supply Risks

Supply disruptions are defined as "unplanned and unanticipated events that disrupt the normal flow of goods and materials within the supply chain". They distinguish between coordination risks and disruption risks. Supply chain complexity is described by Adenso-Diaz et al. (2012) as "the sum of the total number of nodes and the total number of forward, backward and within-tier material flows" in the upstream supply chain network. Such complexity has a huge impact on supply chain reliability and supply chain stability. The overall recommendation made in several papers is to reduce the number of suppliers, since supply chain complexity increases the risk of disruption. Adenso-Diaz et al. (2012) highlighted the definitions of various authors, using a variety of criteria: (1) function, (2) type of risk, (3) drivers of risks, and (4) likelihood of occurrence. While the literature on supply management and risk management is growing, there is no organized structure regarding the sources of causal factors for supply chain risks and supply disruptions. Several papers show that supply disruptions can lead to high monetary recovery cost, waste, and sharp decreases in sales as pointed out in one of the previous sections by Haslett (2011), Jing (2011), and Grant (2010). As well as findings in literature, other sources such as field research, internal reports, and interviews display that supply disruptions have severe impacts on companies in the analysed European transportation industry. Supply disruptions and their associated risks have been classified in the literature using a variety of criteria, e.g. function (Christopher and Peck 2004), type of risk, and drivers of risk (Chopra and Sodhi 2004). Pointed out that enterprises without operational slack and redundancies in their supply chains experience negative stock effects. They also revealed the tremendous impacts of supply chain disruptions on stock price performance and shareholder value. Causal factors for supply disruptions are automatically associated with risks in the supply network, as stated by Zsidisin (2003). Several authors outline incidents in which supply disruptions caused production standstill or temporary stops in manufacturing companies in the European industry. Other authors refer to capacity management in terms of supply disruptions as being a crucial risk factor for supply chain discrepancies. Due to such risks, specific measures are necessary in terms of overcoming potential supply disruptions caused by supplier capacity shortages (Hittle and Leonard 2011). Mitigations and preventive measures can take the form of diverse capacity management, back-up equipment, or alternative manufacturing locations, as recommended by Hittle and Leonard (2011).

It is useful to compare the supply chain strategies of companies and their resulting ability to cope with some of the abovementioned disruptions. Zsidisin (2003) created models which can be used by managers to measure and assess the vulnerability of their company and supply chain in relation to the associated risks. Typology may also provide avenues for future research and thus guide practitioners in the management of their supply chain risk portfolio. Such a classification is a useful tool for supply chain managers in differentiating between independent and dependent variables and the mutual relationships which would help them to focus on those key variables that are most important for effective risk minimization in a supply chain. Zsidisin typologized causal factors for supply disruptions into different categories – high, medium, and low risk – based on managerial perception. Other authors besides Zsidian have built on this typology and outlined causal factors for supply disruptions as follows, which comprise the:

- Capacity shortages
- New product launches
- Disaster issues (e.g. earthquake, flood)
- Lack of supply chain transparency
- Labour-related issues (e.g. strike)
- Constraints on market capacity
- Pricing instabilities
- Quality discrepancies
- Transport issues
- Product transfers to sites or plants
- Inflexible production capacities

10.3.6 Method of Evaluation

Once a company has decided what it is going to evaluate, the next step is to establish how it will evaluate the performance of the supplier. There are many ways to do this, and some are more costly, time-consuming, and resource intensive than others. By quantifying the level of risk and the projected benefit of a method of evaluation, company personnel can determine the most appropriate method or combination of methods that should be used. Some methods that companies commonly use to evaluate and measure supplier performance include (Figs. 10.6 and 10.7):

- Site visits by cross-functional teams

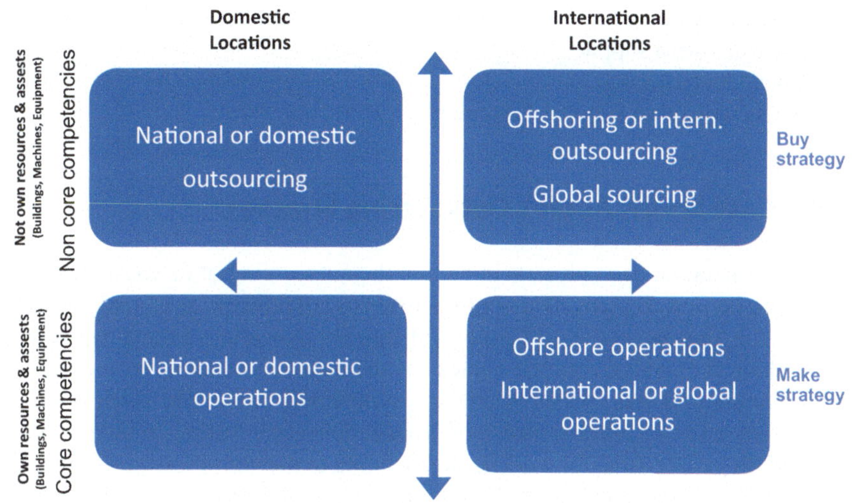

Fig. 10.6 Make-or-buy strategy. (Source: Author's source)

	Own Production Make	External Procurement or Outsourcing Buy
Definition	▪ Own production or acquisition until now ▪ Externally rendered performances	▪ Procurement from suppliers or outsourcing until now ▪ Internally rendered performances for third parties
Advantages Chances	▪ Less dependency regarding costs ▪ Quality and flexibility ▪ Possibly less coordination effort ▪ Utilisation of existing capacities	▪ Concentration on core business ▪ Know-how utilisation of experienced partners ▪ Quality improvement through professionalization ▪ Reduction of complexity in the processes ▪ Growth in flexibility and short-term ▪ capacity availability ▪ Quicker reaction ability to changes ▪ Market changes ▪ Cost reduction potential through scale effects of ▪ suppliers/outsourcing recipient ▪ Flexible access to capacities worldwide
Disvantages Risks	▪ Higher investment & warranty risk ▪ Higher commitment	▪ High costs for change of supplier ▪ Loss of product identification ▪ Loss of control over externally procured/outsourced tasks ▪ Knowledge drain

Fig. 10.7 Advantages and disadvantages of make and buy strategies. (Source: Author's source)

- Supplier audits (process, special process, or product audits)
- Paper supplier questionnaires
- Web-based supplier questionnaires
- Organizing existing data
- Internal questionnaires
- Requiring external certifications
- Developing own certifications

- Third-party reviews
- Phone call with a supplier
- Independent ratings
- Contacts with other supplier customers

10.4 Case Study: Apple's Outsourcing Strategy

Apple's commercial triumph rests in part on the outsourcing of its consumer electronics production to Asia. Drawing on extensive fieldwork at China's leading exporter, the Taiwanese-owned Foxconn, the power dynamics of the buyer-driven supply chain are analysed in the context of the national terrains that mediate or even accentuate global pressures. Power asymmetries assure the dominance of Apple in price setting and the timing of product delivery, resulting in intense pressures and illegal overtime for workers. Responding to the high-pressure production regime, the young generation of Chinese rural migrant workers engages in a crescendo of individual and collective struggles to define their rights and defend their dignity in the face of combined corporate and state power. As the principal manufacturer of products and components for Apple, Taiwanese company Foxconn currently employs 1.4 million workers in China alone. Arguably, then, just as Apple has achieved a globally dominant position, described as "the world's most valuable brand", so too have the fortunes of Foxconn been entwined with Apple's success, facilitating Foxconn's rise to become the world's largest electronics contractor (Van der Pijl 2015). Figure 10.8 shows the employees and the location of factories in China for Apple iPhone and iPad production.

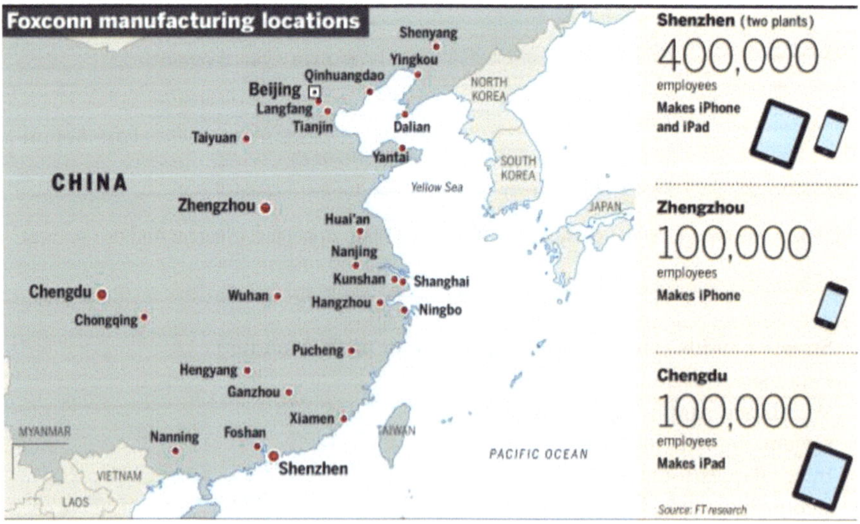

Fig. 10.8 Foxconn's manufacturing sites for Apple

Fig. 10.9 International supply negotiations. (Source: Author's source)

Figure 10.9 shows Ann Sun, Manager Supplier Development, and the General Manager, Dr. Marc Helmold, in Japan. The visit served to integrate a Japanese supplier into the Bombardier supply network.

References

Aberdeen Group. (2005). *Assuring supply and mitigating risks in an uncertain economy. Supply Risk Management Benchmark*. Boston: Aberdeen Group.

Adenso-Diaz, B., Mena, C. H., Garcia, S., & Liechty, M. (2012). Supply chain management: The impact of supply network characteristics on reliability. *An International Journal, 17*(3), 1–36.

Christopher, M., & Peck, H. (2004). Building the resilient chain. *International Journal of Logistics Management, 15*(2), 1–5.

Dust, R., Gleiser, M., & Gürtler, B. (2010). Total Supplier Risk Monitoring. Lieferfähigkeit präventiv absichern. *MQ, Magazine for Quality and Management*, 1–2, 27-29.

Dyer, J. H. (1996). Specialized supplier networks as a source of competitive advantage: Evidence from the auto industry. *Strategic Management Journal, 17*(4), 271–291.

Emmett, St. & Crocker, B. (2009). *Excellence in Supplier Management. How to better manage contracts with suppliers and add value. Best practices in Supplier Relationship and Supplier Development*. Cambridge: Cambridge Academic.

Gürtler, B., & Spinler, S. (2010). A network-oriented investigation of supply risk and implications to supply risk monitoring. *International Journal of Production, 12*, 1–27.

Grant, D. (2010). Honda recall airbags: Recall expands to another 438,000 vehicles. The *Christian Science Monitor*. October 28th, 2012, Retrieved from http://www.csmonitor.com/Business/2010/0210/Honda-recall-airbags-Recall-expands-to-another-438-000-vehicles.

Haslett, E. (2011). Eurostar back on the rails despite snow outage. October 28th, 2012, Retrieved from http://www.managementtoday.co.zuk/news/1049498/Eurostar-back-rails-despite-snow-outage/

Helmold, M. (2014). *Establishing a best practice model of supplier relationship management (SRM) for multinational manufacturing companies in the European transportation industry*. Berlin: Wissenschaftlicher Verlag.

Helmold, M., Dathe, T., Hummel, F., Terry, B., & Pieper, J. (2020). *Successful international negotiations. A practical guide for managing transactions and deals. Management for professionals*. Heidelberg: Springer.

Hittle, B., & Leonard, K. M. (2011). Decision making in advance of a supply chain crisis. *Management Decision, 49*(7), 1182–1193.

Hofbauer, G., et al. (2012). *Lieferantenmanagement. Die wertorientierte Gestaltung der Lieferbeziehung* (2nd ed.). Munich: Oldenbourg Verlag.

Jing, J. (2011). *China's new high-Speed rail plagued by power outages*. Epoch Times. October 28th, 2012. Retrieved from http://m.theepochtimes.com/n2/china-news/chinas-new-high-speed-rail-plagued-by-power-outages-59023.html

Kuerble, P., Helmold, M., Bode, O. H., & Scholz, U. (2016). *Beschaffung-Produktion-Marketing*. Marburg: Tectum.

Ohnoe, T. (1990). Das Toyota-Produktions system. Frankfurt: Campus-Verlag.

Porter, M. E. (1985). *Competitive Advantage. Creating and sustaining superior Performance*. Free Press New York.

Slack, N. et al. (1995). *Operations Management*. London: Pitman Publishing.

Trkman, P., & McCormack, K. (2009). Supply chain risks in turbulent environments – A conceptual model for supply chain network risk. *International Journal of Production Economics, 119*(2), 247–258.

Van der Pijl, K. (2015). *Handbook of international economics and production*. Cheltenham: Elgar.

Zsidisin, G. A. (2003). Managerial perceptions of supply risk. *Journal of Supply Chain Management, 39*(1), 14–25.

11 Lean Management on the Downstream (Demand Side)

Progress is impossible without the ability to admit mistakes. Kaizen means ongoing improvement involving everybody, without spending much money. You can't do kaizen just once or twice and expect immediate results. You have to be in it for the long haul.

Masaaki Imai (1930-today)

11.1 Lean Management on Demand Side

In the present competitive market environment, it is important to apply lean tools across the supply chain. Lean concepts provide supply chain agility to produce and deliver products in a flexible, timely, and cost-effective manner with the highest quality standards (Helmold and Samara 2019).

11.1.1 Efficient Consumer Response (ECR)

ECR (Efficient Consumer Response) is a strategy to increase the level of services to consumers through close cooperation among retailers, wholesalers, and manufacturers. By aiming to improve the efficiency of a supply chain as a whole beyond the wall of retailers, wholesalers, and manufacturers, they can consequently gain larger profits than each of them pursuing their own business goals. Companies who compose the supply chain can reduce the opportunity loss, inventory level, and entire cost, as well as increase monetary profitability by sharing the purpose of "customer satisfaction". "ECR" is a strategic concept compiled by a consulting firm "Kurt Simon Associates" at the request of organizations concerning the US processed food distribution industry, aiming to recover the competitive strength for surviving the turbulent time of the industry when discounters emerged in the USA. For "ECR",

M. Helmold, *Lean Management and Kaizen*, Management for Professionals,
https://doi.org/10.1007/978-3-030-46981-8_11

reengineering such as eliminating or adding business operations is performed by checking all business operations of a supply chain of companies by a criterion of whether they contribute to providing higher values to consumers. This aims to provide better convenience, better products, better quality, and better selection of goods and build a "win-win" relationship among companies concerned (i.e. every company of a supply chain wins and gains profits). The first target of ECR is to reengineer business processes. To realize the reengineering, information technology such as EDI (Electronic Data Interchange) that is used for accurate and timely exchange of information between companies is necessary. Characteristic of ECR is that reengineering is performed considering final results given to consumers from unified business processes and that can be realized by information technology.

11.1.2 Vendor-Managed Inventory (VMI)

Vendor-managed inventory (VMI) is a concept and business models in which the customer of a product range discloses information in terms of production planning, forecasts, and demands to the suppliers (vendor) of those products in order to enable the supplier takes full responsibility for maintaining an agreed inventory quantity of the material, usually at the buyer's warehouse. In many industries, the VMI is managed for a number of suppliers. VMI will thus help suppliers to optimize material and production in line with customer tact and to deliver material in sequence to the assembly line on request.

11.1.3 Enterprise Resource Planning Integration (ERP)

Enterprise resource planning (ERP) is defined as the ability to deliver an integrated suite of business applications. ERP tools share a common process and data model, covering broad and deep operational end-to-end processes, such as those found in finance, HR, distribution, manufacturing, service, and the supply chain.

11.1.4 Quick Response (QR)

Quick response manufacturing (QRM) is an approach to manufacturing which emphasizes the beneficial effect of reducing internal and external lead times. Quick response manufacturing (QRM) idea aims at permanent restructuring of manufacturing processes and continuous adjustment of actions to interior and exterior changes. The quick response manufacturing conception is, in a way, a modification of previous systems. Moreover, QRM is apparently directed to compress time in all the action spheres and delivery chains of a company. Its implementation not only ensures effective time management inside a company but also strengthens cooperation between suppliers and recipients. Besides, it also ensures a flexible reaction to market signals and improves competitiveness of a company in the long term. During the last few years, many of the

US companies have implemented the QRM strategy, which has given astounding results (Suri and Krishnamurthy 2003). The typical results were shortening the lead time (80–95percent both in the stages of production and planning/administration), lowering product costs (15–50percent), quality improvement of delivery realization (40–98percent), as well as better exploitation of materials and a decreased number of corrections (80percent). QRM has achieved these results owing to detailed management rules, production methods, analysis techniques, and tools. Additionally, QRM takes an extra effort to shorten the time of launching the product into the market.

11.1.5 Incoterms 2020

The International Chamber of Commerce (ICC) in Paris has been issuing "International Rules for the Interpretation of Commercial Contract Formulas" known as Incoterms (International Commercial Terms) since 1923. The Incoterms rules have become an essential part of the daily language of international trade. They have been incorporated in contracts for the sale of goods worldwide and provide rules and guidance to importers, exporters, lawyers, transporters, insurers, and students of international trade. After ICC's creation in 1919, one of its first initiatives was to facilitate international trade activities. In the early 1920s, the world business organization set out to understand the commercial trade terms used by merchants. This was done through a study that was limited to 6 commonly used terms in just 13 countries. The findings were published in 1923, highlighting disparities in interpretation. To examine the discrepancies identified in the initial survey, a second study was carried out. This time, the scope was expanded to the interpretation of trade terms used in more than 30 countries in 1928. Based on the findings of the studies, the first version of the Incoterms rules was published as a global standard. The terms included FAS, FOB, C&F, CIF, Ex Ship, and Ex Quay. Due to World War II, supplementary revisions of the Incoterms rules were suspended and did not resume again until the 1950s. The first revision of the Incoterms rules was then issued in 1953. It debuted three new trade terms for non-maritime transport. The new rules comprised DCP (Delivered Costs Paid), FOR (Free on Rail), and FOT (Free on Truck). The ICC launched the third revision of the Incoterms rules, which dealt with misinterpretations of the previous version. Two trade terms were added to address delivery at frontier (DAF) and delivery at destination (DDP). The increased use of air transportation gave cause for another version of the popular trade terms. This edition included the new term FOB Airport (Free on Board Airport). This rule aimed to allay confusion around the term FOB (Free on Board) by signifying the exact "vessel" used. With the expansion of carriage of goods in containers and new documentation processes came the need for another revision. This edition introduced the trade term FRC (Free Carrier at Named Point), which provided for goods not actually received by the ship's side but at a reception point on shore, such as a container yard. The fifth revision simplified the Free Carrier term by deleting rules for specific modes of transport (i.e. FOR, Free on Rail; FOT, Free on Truck; and FOB Airport, Free on Board Airport). It was considered sufficient to use the general term FCA (Free Carrier at Named Point) instead. Other provisions accounted for increased use of electronic messages. The "License, Authorizations and Formalities" section of FAS and DEQ Incoterms rules was modified to comply with the way most customs authorities address the issues of exporter and importer of record. The Incoterms 2020 is the most current edition of the rules to date. This version consolidated the D-family of rules, removing DAF (Delivered at Frontier), DES (Delivered Ex Ship), DEQ (Delivered Ex Quay), and DDU (Delivered Duty Unpaid) and adding DAT (Delivered at Terminal) and DAP (Delivered at Place). Other modifications included an increased obligation for buyer and seller to cooperate on information sharing and changes to accommodate "string sales". To keep pace with the ever-evolving global trade landscape, the latest update to the trade terms is currently in progress and is set to be unveiled in 2020. The Incoterms 2020 Drafting Group includes lawyers, traders, and company representatives from around the world. The overall process will take 2 years as practical input on what works and what could possibly be improved will be collected from a range of Incoterms rules users worldwide and studied (Table 11.1).

11.2 Case Study: Huawei Manufacturing Strategy 2025

Automation in factories isn't new. Today, though, the disruptive force of digital transformation is taking manufacturing far beyond automation. Industry 4.0, mass customization, and advances in tech like 3D printing and nanomaterials have placed humanity at the cusp of several game changers when it comes to this US$11.6-trillion industry (Maidment 2016). Automation began back in the 1800s with mechanized cotton spinners, steam power, and the arrival of the first industrial revolution. By the 1930s, the automotive industry was leading the second industrial revolution of mass production, paving the way for the digital control systems of the 1970s. In the 1980s, car makers became intensive adopters of industrial robots, at which point computers and automation were embodying the third industrial revolution.

Table 11.1 International commercial terms 2020 (incoterms)

Abbreviations	Description (English/German)
EXW	Ex Works/Ab Werk
FCA	Free Carrier/Frei Frachtführer
FAS	Free Alongside Ship/Frei Längsseite Schiff
FOB	Free on Board/Frei an Bord
CFR	Cost and Freight/Kosten und Fracht
CIF	Cost, Insurance, and Freight/Kosten, Versicherung und Fracht
CPT	Carriage Paid To/Frachtfrei
CIP	Carriage, Insurance Paid To/Frachtfrei versichert
DAP	Delivered at Place/Geliefert benannter Ort
DAT	Delivered at Terminal/Geliefert Terminal
DDP	Delivered Duty Paid/Geliefert verzollt

Source: Author's own table, adopted from Helmold and Terry (2016)

Jump forward to more recent milestones, Foxconn in China was running up to ten automated production lines in some of its factories by the end of 2016, in the second of its three-phase full automation plan. Also in 2016, Adidas unveiled its first fully robot-built sneaker, 1 of 500 planned prototypes for its new factory in Germany. Though we're not quite there yet, the arrival of lights-out manufacturing is a case of when, not if.

Automation is certainly not new, but digital transformation is so much more than robots assembling parts – it's destined to disrupt every link in the manufacturing value chain and virtually lead us into the fourth industrial revolution: the cyber-physical age. As data takes centre stage, connectivity and cloud, big data and IoT, and AI and virtualization will act in concert to create a new business paradigm.

But, there's a problem: manufacturing enterprises have been sluggish when it comes to embracing digitalization.

Germany's Industry 4.0 might still draw a blank-face response from some business leaders, but it represents the next phase in manufacturing in Europe. Equivalents are the Industrial Internet in the USA and Made in China 2025. All involve the convergence of a range of technological enablers and accelerators, the result of which will be connected, smart factories and smart manufacturing.

Smart manufacturing goes beyond computing and automation. It creates a cyber-physical system, or digital twin, as a virtual model of a process, product, or service. Underpinned by ubiquitous, low-latency connectivity in the shape of 5G, smart sensors transmit data to the cloud where it's processed and analysed to give contextual and predictive data.

Pairing a physical and virtual world has several advantages. GE Digital's Denzil Samuels explains one advantage using the example of a jet engine on which smart sensors constantly transmit enough data to build a cyber copy, "The engine that's now being simulated can take over the pain of major aircraft engine maintenance by replacing a single blade that's worn as soon as we know about it. Or better still, predicting when it'll get worn to the point when it needs replacing, so we can minimize the amount of time that the engine is actually out of commission".

Moreover, the connectivity afforded by smart manufacturing links all processes from R&D, sourcing materials, and production to QA, sales, distribution, and logistics.

Over the next decade, smart manufacturing will extend past individual factories to connect groups of factories and the manufacturing industry with other verticals.

The convergence of manufacturing and services will continue with the XaaS model based on IoT and data insights. Thus, the services that manufacturers will require and deliver based on the products they make will increase, many of which will be driven by data insights and consumer demand. In the B2C space, consumers in emerging economies will become a dominant market presence, while demand in developed countries will fragment. However, customization in products and after-sales services is likely to increase.

3D printing will evolve from prototyping to a viable means of mass production in the 2020s. Advances in raw materials will enhance parts' design, manufacturing processes, and printing technology. At the same time, the use of nanomaterials, which we're seeing today in products like clothing, sports goods, and electronics, will expand into an industry worth US$170 billion a year. Coupled with improvements in robotics and AI, new areas of demand will emerge.

Back to 2017, and C-suite executives need to consider how maturing technologies like AI, virtualization, and 3D printing will shape the future, alongside the connected manufacturing ecosystem of Industry 4.0 plus changing market dynamics. Despite advances in technology, we live in uncertain times. Strategic investment in digital infrastructure, skilled staff, and partnerships are the tools to make things happen in the next decade of smart disruption.

References

Helmold, M., & Samara, W. (2019). *Progress in performance management. Industry insights and case studies on principles, application tools, and practice*. Heidelberg: Springer.

Helmold, M., & Terry, B. (2016). Lieferantenmanagement 2030: Wertschöpfung und Sicherung der Wettbewerbsfähigkeit in digitalen und globalen Märkten. Springer Wiesbaden.

Maidment, G. (2016). Huawei. Smart manufacturing: More than just robots. Retrieved 22.11.2019. https://www.huawei.com/au/about-huawei/publications/winwin-magazine/plus-intelligence/smart-manufacturing-more-than-robots

Suri R., & Krishnamurthy A. (2003). How to plan and implement POLCA: A material control system for high-variety or custom-engineered products. Technical report. Center for the quick response manufacturing.

Lean Management KPI and OKR

12

Data is of course important in manufacturing, but I place the greatest emphasis on facts.

Taiichi Ohno (1912–1990)

12.1 The Lean Performance Management Cycle

Lean management must be an integral part of any enterprise and organization. Performance improvements and permanent adjustments are important factors for the successful implementation of lean structures. Performance management therefore integrates a cycle from performance measurement and analysis (Plan), the performance action and implementation (Do), the performance management controlling (Check), and the performance improvements and adjustments (Act) as illustrated in the lean performance management cycle in Fig. 12.1. The figure shows the lean performance management cycle as an iterative and continuous process for the control and improvement of processes, products, or services. The original P-D-C-A four-step framework is also known as Deming circle.

PM is a basic and efficient methodology. It portrays the administration of enterprises, processes, HR, divisions, and associations to ensure that objectives and destinations are being reached. The objectives and destinations are gotten from client's desires which are the bases of the key mission and vision in an endeavour. Performance measurement and the administration must be executed over the whole value chain and applies to all functions and department (Helmold et al. 2019). PM reaches from the upstream value chain over the operation to the downstream supply chain management. Performance management involves defining what effective performance looks like, as developing the tools and procedures necessary to measure performance. The overall goal of performance management is to ensure that the organization and all of its subsystems (processes, departments, teams, employees,

M. Helmold, *Lean Management and Kaizen*, Management for Professionals,
https://doi.org/10.1007/978-3-030-46981-8_12

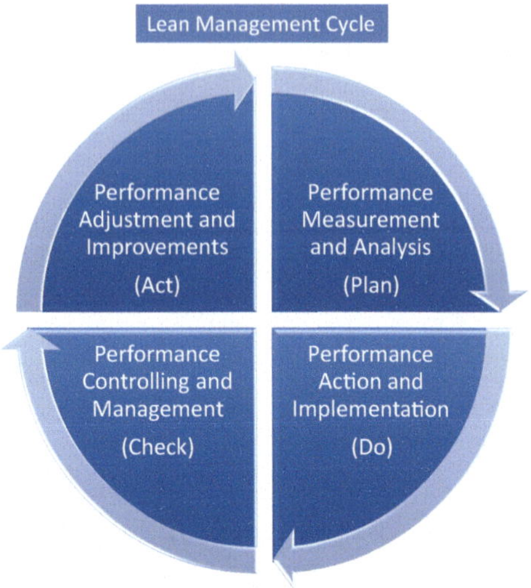

Fig. 12.1 Lean performance excellence. (Source: Author)

etc.) are working together in an optimum fashion to achieve the results desired by the organization.

Performance management can be done externally (e.g. measurement by customers, by shareholders or analysts, measurement of supply base) and internally (management of organization). PM must include the entire value chain and all elements including USCM, operations, DSCM, and support functions like finance, logistics, human resources (HR), or information technology (IT). Purely financial PM is not successful, so that all stakeholders and functions have to integrate and collaborate in order to achieve the excellent performance. The key questions related to performance management are:

- What is performance management?
- Where do I measure performance?
- What do I measure?
- How can I measure performance?
- When do I measure performance?
- How can I improve the performance?

Enterprises must aim for PM excellence. Permanent measurement and improvements are crucial activities by top management. PM is a core activity and must be pursued by all departments. In addition, there are certain characteristics of PM that can be described as follows (Fig. 12.2):

1. PM has to be executed over the entire value chain from the upstream over the operation to the downstream supply chain management.
2. PM is a structural and systematic approach in enterprises and organization.
3. PM must be coordinated and implemented by top management.

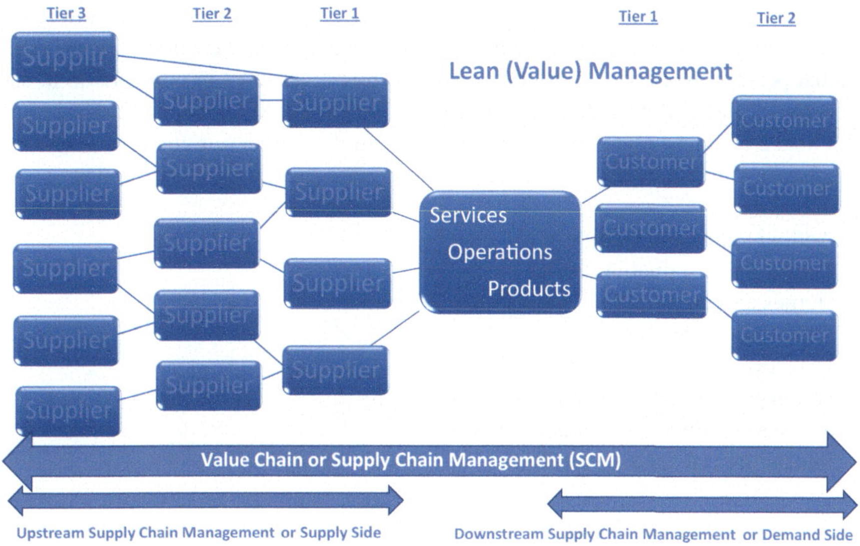

Fig. 12.2 Lean management across the value chain. (Source: Author)

4. PM deals with enterprises, processes, employees, departments, and organizations.
5. PM is using tools, mechanics, and procedures necessary to measure performance (BSC, Audits, or EFQM).
6. PM goals and objectives to perform efficiently and effectively.
7. PM goals are relevant to customer and stakeholder expectations.
8. PM goals and objectives are derived from customer's (and stakeholder) expectations which are the bases of the strategic mission and vision.
9. PM uses qualitative and quantitative measurables and key performance indicators (KPI).
10. PM strives for excellence and permanent improvements.

12.2 Lean Performance Excellence

Performance excellence can be defined as achieving and maintaining outstanding and superior levels of performance that meet and exceed the expectations of the stakeholders (Helmold and Samara 2019). There are a huge number of stakeholders for any business or enterprise, and to be assessed as excellent, these enterprises have to be achieving an outstanding level of performance for all of their different stakeholders: employees, customers, shareholders, owners, and the wider community. To achieve sustained and superior levels of excellence, it is mandatory for enterprises and organizations to permanently assess the situation and to strive for improvement by initiating continuous improvement programmes like the Toyota production system or excellence models.

Excellence model allows the management of enterprises and organizations to understand the cause and effect relationships between what their organization does (actual performance), the enablers, and the results it achieves in comparison to set objectives (plan). The model comprises three integrated components. Fundamental excellence concepts underlie principles that form the foundation for achieving sustainable excellence in any organization. These principles can be described as:

- Adding value for customers
- Creating a sustainable future
- Harnessing creativity and innovation
- Managing with agility
- Developing organizational capability
- Leading with vision, inspiration, and integrity
- Succeeding through the talent of people
- Sustaining outstanding results

The goal of any excellence initiative and programme must therefore be to achieve world-class excellence as illustrated in Fig. 12.3. The system, developed by Dr. Marc Helmold, is similar to the German school grading system (1 = very good, 5 = failed). Companies usually start as so-called laggards (Level 5) (Helmold et al. 2019). A laggard can be defined as organization that falls behind similar companies in the same industry. The next level is a "standard" performance (Level 4). Standard means in this context that enterprises have an average performance level in a certain sector. The next level is "maturity" in performance including some best practices (Level 3). After the maturity organizations will achieve the "industry excellence" (Level 2) level. In this level, performance is outstanding within the industry. The last

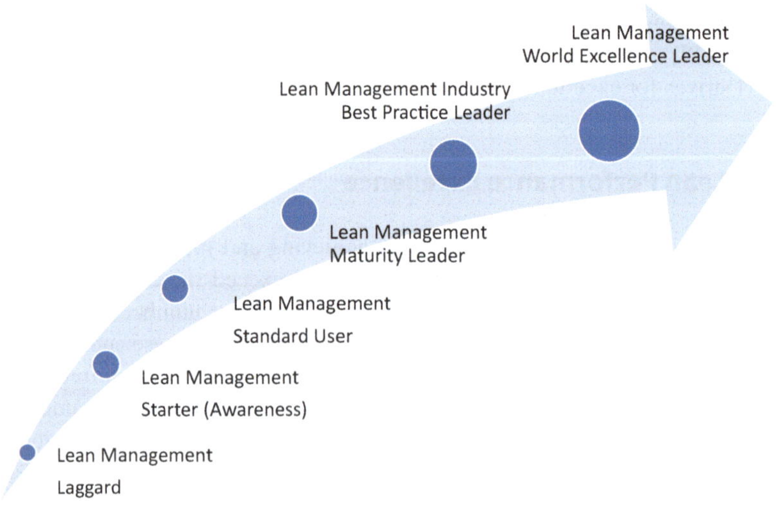

Fig. 12.3 Lean management excellence. (Source: Author's own figure)

and highest level is the world class excellence level, in which organizations are benchmarks in terms of excellence on a global scale (Level 1) (Helmold et al. 2019).

12.3 Key Performance Indicators (KPI)

Key performance indicators (KPI) are a set of quantifiable measures that a company uses to gauge its performance over time. These metrics are used to determine a company's progress in achieving its strategic and operational goals and also to compare a company's finances and performance against other businesses within its industry. A key performance indicator (KPI) is a measure of your performance against key business objectives. High-level KPIs may focus on the overall performance of the enterprise, while low-level KPIs may focus on processes or employees in departments such as sales, marketing, or a call centre.

12.4 Objective Key Results (OKR)

The OKR system is a performance tool that sets, communicates, and monitors goals in an organization so that all employees work together in one direction. The development of OKRs is generally attributed to Andy Grove, the "Father of OKRs", who introduced the approach to Intel during his tenure there and documented this in his 1983 book *High Output Management*. Objectives and key results (OKR) is a popular leadership process for setting, communicating, and monitoring quarterly goals and results in organizations. The goal of OKRs is to connect company, team, and personal objectives in a hierarchical way to measurable results, making all employees work together in one unified direction, by using the SMART-objective methodology. OKRs consist of a list of three to five high-level objectives. Under each objective then usually three to five key measurable results are listed. Each key result has a progress indicator or score of 0 to 100 percent or 0 to 1.0 that shows its achievement. The advantages can be outlined as follows:

Goal focused company alignment: align with your leadership team on top priorities and highest leverage activities each quarter

Fit Objectives into company vision, mission, and values to motivate your company with purpose

Visibility into company, department and individual progress, wins, and road blocked areas

KPIs are important for the plant floor because they are highly effective for exposing, quantifying, and visualizing muda (the lean term for waste); and they are also highly effective motivators. The essence of lean manufacturing and the central theme of the Toyota production system are to eliminate waste – to relentlessly eliminate all activities that do not add value for your customer. Effective KPIs quantify waste; provide an early warning system for processes operating outside the norm; and offer important hints to where improvement efforts should be focused.

KPIs also function as very effective motivators. Motivation theory is a complex field with many diverse opinions. However, there is wide agreement that a central key to effective motivation is setting challenging but attainable goals (e.g. SMART goals, which are specific, measurable, achievable, realistic, and time-specific). SMART goals are ideal candidates for plant floor KPIs.

For example, a manufacturing plant with semi-automated processes introduced real-time visual KPIs as a means of motivating their operators. One of their engineers mistakenly set the expected run rate for a cell at 180 pieces per minute instead of the normal 140 pieces per minute. Hours later the engineer returned and was astonished to find the cell averaging 178 pieces per minute. Visual KPIs had motivated the operators to greatly exceed what the process engineers had thought was possible.

There is a connection between the two real-time KPI perspectives: the lean manufacturing perspective of eliminating waste and the corporate perspective of achieving strategic goals. They are connected through waste.

From a broad lean perspective, the seven major forms of waste in the manufacturing process include the TIMWOOD model. The model shows how objectives can be defined:

- Transport: distance, time
- Inventory: money, quantity
- Motion: time
- Waiting: time, number of operators waiting, place of waiting
- Overproduction: number of goods, money for overproduced goods, employees involved
- Overprocessing: employees involved
- Defects: number of defects, money (loss cost)

12.5 Case Study: Microsoft's Strategy and Objectives

Fiscal year 2019 was a record-breaking year for Microsoft. They achieved more than $125 billion in revenues and $43 billion in operating income and more than $50 billion in operating cash flow (Microsoft 2019). The enterprise returned more than $30 billion to its shareholders. The commercial cloud business is the largest in the world, surpassing $38 billion in revenue for the year, with gross margin expanding to 63 percent. Consumers, students, teachers, and more than 2 billion first-line workers around the world are using Microsoft products. The mission statement to empower every person and every organization on the planet to achieve more is one of the key elements in the strategy of Microsoft. Microsoft IT platforms and tools enable small businesses to be more productive, multinationals to be more competitive, nonprofit organizations to be more effective, and governments to be more efficient. At present, Microsoft is a technology company, and every organization will increasingly need to build its own proprietary technology solutions to compete and grow. The organization embraces this approach to adopt best-in-class software and services but also build their own digital capability. Computing is becoming embedded in the world, in every place and everything. This era of the intelligent cloud and intelligent edge is shaping the next phase of innovation, powering intelligent systems and experiences that previously would have been unimaginable, and transforming nearly everything around us. Across Microsoft's businesses, we are innovating to empower our customers and investing in large and growing markets to help them digitally transform.

Applications and Infrastructure In a world where every company is a digital company, developers will play an increasingly vital role in value creation and growth across every industry, and GitHub is their home. Since the acquisition of GitHub last fall, growth has accelerated. Today it's used by more than 40 million developers, including those who work at the majority of the Fortune 50. Microsoft is building Azure as the world's computer, addressing customers' real-world operational sovereignty and regulatory needs. Today, 95 percent of the Fortune 500 trust Azure for their mission-critical workloads.

Data and AI The variety, velocity, and volume of data is increasing – with 50 billion connected devices coming online by 2030, more than double the number today – and Azure is the only cloud with limitless data and analytics capabilities across our customers' entire data estate. We brought hyperscale capabilities to our relational database services for the first time this year, and we offer the most comprehensive cloud analytics – from Azure Data Factory to Azure SQL Data Warehouse to Power BI. The quintessential characteristic for every application going forward will be AI, and we believe it cannot be the exclusive province of a few companies or countries. That's why we are democratizing AI infrastructure, tools, and services with Azure Cognitive Services, so any developer can embed the ability to see, hear, respond, translate, reason, and more into their applications. Azure Cognitive Services is the most comprehensive portfolio of AI tools available, and this year, we added new speech-to-text, search, vision, and decision capabilities, as well as updates to Azure Machine Learning to streamline the building, training, and deployment of machine learning models.

Business Applications Dynamics 365 uniquely enables any organization to create digital feedback loops that take data from one system and use it to optimize the outcomes of another, enabling any business to become AI-first. This year, we introduced Dynamics 365 AI, a new class of AI application built for an era where systems of record and engagement are converted into intelligence. And the Open Data Initiative we launched with Adobe and SAP last fall takes this even further, delivering on our vision to enable data to be exchanged and enriched across systems to provide unparalleled business insight.

Microsoft is enabling our customers to digitize not only their business processes but to bridge the physical and digital worlds with our investments in mixed-reality cloud. The new HoloLens 2 is the most advanced, intelligent edge device available, offering two times the field of view and three times the comfort as the previous version. And, together with Dynamics 365 and new Azure mixed-reality services, it enables organizations to digitize physical spaces and interactions and empower their first-line employees with the right information at the right time, in the context of their work.

LinkedIn now has more than 645 million members and is the most comprehensive solution for every organization to manage and engage their most important resource – their talent. Our Talent portfolio – from Talent Solutions and Talent Insights, to employee engagement with Glint and LinkedIn Learning – enables every organization to attract, retain, and develop the best talent in an increasingly competitive jobs market.

Modern Workplace Microsoft 365 empowers everyone – enterprises, small businesses, and first-line workers – with an integrated, secure experience that transcends any one device. We are helping every business build out their system of communication and collaboration to drive their productivity as well as their business transformation. We are infusing AI across Microsoft 365 to enable new automation, prediction, translation, and insights capabilities. Meetings are more inclusive in Microsoft Teams, presentations more accessible in PowerPoint, videos more searchable in Stream, and emails more relevant in Outlook. And with Workplace Analytics and Microsoft Search, we distil knowledge and insights from data to help people work smarter, not longer. Office 365 Commercial has 180 million users. Our EMS install base exceeded 100 million. And the Outlook apps on iOS and Android also surpassed more than 100 million users for the first time.

Gaming In gaming, Microsoft is pursuing our expansive opportunity to transform how games are distributed, played, and viewed. Our new breakthrough game streaming technology, Project xCloud, will enter public trials this fall. It will put gamers at the centre of their gaming experience, enabling them to play games in high-fidelity wherever and whenever they want, on any device.

Microsoft Game Stack brings together our tools and services to empower game developers – from independent creators to the biggest game studios – to build, operate, and scale cloud-first games across mobile, PC, and console. Our growing Xbox Live community is key to our approach, and for the first time we are enabling developers to reach these highly engaged gamers on iOS and Android. Finally, we increased our first-party game studios to 15 this year to deliver differentiated content for our fast-growing subscription services like Xbox Game Pass, which is now available on both console and PC.

CSR Beyond these three pillars, we are working to foster a sustainable future where everyone has access to the benefits and opportunities created by technology.

As a reflection of the importance we place on advancing environmental and social progress, Microsoft's board of directors has a Regulatory and Public Policy Committee that works together with me, my leadership team, and others across Microsoft to oversee our commitments to environmental sustainability and corporate social responsibility. No single company is going to solve macro challenges like climate change alone, but as a global technology company, we are well-positioned to enable and accelerate digital transformations that lead to a low-carbon future. That is why we are stepping up our commitment. Over the past year, we expanded our work through our operations, investments, partnerships, and advocacy across initiatives spanning both environmental and social responsibility.

We continue to operate carbon neutral across our worldwide operations, driven by an internal carbon tax, as we have every year since 2012. And we've taken new steps over the past year to align our carbon-reduction efforts with the latest climate science by setting a goal to reduce our operational emissions by 75 percent by 2030, which puts us on a path to exceed the ambitions of the Paris Accord two decades ahead of schedule. This year, we raised our carbon fee to $15 per metric ton, a near doubling of the previous fee, to put sustainability at the core of every part of our business. We're also extending our carbon reduction targets beyond our own operations. We will cut carbon emissions by 30 percent across our global supply chain by 2030. And in October, we extended our carbon-neutrality commitment to our products and devices with a pilot to make 825,000 Xbox consoles carbon neutral.

We are committed to ensuring our datacentres are among the most sustainable in the world. By the end of this year, we will achieve our target of powering our datacentres with 60 percent renewable energy and will aim to reach 70 percent renewable energy within the next 4 years. In fact, when I was in Sweden this spring, we announced our plans to build some of the most advanced and sustainable datacentres to date, powered from 100 percent renewable energy and with zero-waste operations.

And, we are also working with our customers and partners to help them use technology to reduce their own environmental footprints and create their own solutions for a more sustainable planet. Our AI for Earth program, as an example, has expanded access to massive environmental data sets that can help others generate valuable insights about the health of our planet, including the conditions of our air, water, land, and the well-being of our wildlife. And it supports organizations that are applying AI to environmental challenges, by helping them harness the full power of cloud computing.

We are working with organizations around the world to enable young people – including those who identify as female and under-represented minorities – with the digital skills required for the future. For example, we are the largest funder of Code.org, which teaches coding skills and reaches students in almost every country.

We know that there is a broadband gap, and that's why, in the USA, our Airband program is using a mixed-technology approach, including TV whitespaces, to connect 3 million people living in unserved rural areas to broadband by 2022. And we're working in more than 20 countries, harnessing this same technology to bring broadband to rural communities elsewhere.

We also know that access to affordable housing is a significant barrier for many, and this year, we launched a major initiative to expand housing options for people who work in the Puget Sound region where we are headquartered. We believe that everyone should be able to choose to live in the community where they work, not just our employees and business partners, but all those who serve the broader community, from teachers and small-business owners to first responders and medical practitioners. It's why we are putting $500 million to work in loans and grants to accelerate the construction of more affordable housing in the region.

Finally, more broadly, we've expanded our support for the nonprofit sector. We work closely with nonprofit organizations to help them accelerate their organizational transformation with technology, and, in fiscal 2019, Microsoft donated or provided discounted software and services worth more than $1.5 billion via Microsoft Philanthropies. Our employees generously donated an additional $170 million (including company match) through our employee giving program to support nonprofits in local communities around the world.

References

Helmold, M., & Samara, W. (2019). *Progress in Performance Management Industry Insights and Case Studies on Principles, Application Tools, and Practice*. Heidelberg: Springer.

Helmold, M., Dathe, T., & Hummel, F. (2019). *Erfolgreiche Verhandlungen – Best-in-Class Empfehlungen für den Verhandlungsdurchbruch*. Wiesbaden: Springer.

Microsoft (2019). www.microsoft. Com.

The Human Side of Lean Management 13

Knowing is not enough; we must apply. Wishing is not enough; we must do.

Johann Wolfgang von Goethe (1749–1832)

13.1 Human Touch in Lean Management

The human factor is one of the most important aspects in the enterprise. Even though machines and artificial intelligence are taking over some work, people are the most crucial element in achieving the company's goals (Helmold and Samara 2019). Management has to enable a human culture, in which problems in the shop floor are understood and can be addressed by employees in order to implement corrective measures (Helmold and Terry 2016). To give the best of their capability and skills, employees must be motivated to do so. Managers must be able to provide a motive or a reason for doing something or make people want to do it. It is of little use for management to prepare elaborate plans or give instructions for carrying out various activities if the people who are supposed to carry out the plans do not to do so, even though they may have to (Kalkis et al. 2019). Human resources have therefore to implement strategy and leadership culture, which centres the employees in the organization and enterprise as shown in Fig. 13.1. A lean culture must address the values of empowerment and autonomous work groups, in which employees can make and propose improvements (Ohno 1990). Clear structures and transparent processes will help to implement this lean culture inside the organization (Liker 2004).

M. Helmold, *Lean Management and Kaizen*, Management for Professionals, https://doi.org/10.1007/978-3-030-46981-8_13

Fig. 13.1 Lean enterprise. (Source: Author's Source)

13.2 Failure Culture and Change Management

The culture of failure in lean management is the combination of shared values, goals, and practices that encourages learning through experimentation and errors. The goal of building this mindset of failure is to create workflows that allow employees to learn from unsuccessful endeavours and to continuously improve processes and activities. Change management is a systematic approach to dealing with the transition or transformation of an organization's goals, processes, or technologies. The purpose of change management is to implement strategies for effecting change, controlling change, and helping people to adapt to change. Change management in lean production utilizes processes, tools, and techniques to manage the people side of change to achieve the required business outcome. Change management incorporates the organizational tools that can be utilized to help individuals make successful personal transitions resulting in the adoption and realization of change. Change management can be used to manage many types of organizational change. The three most common types are:

1. Developmental change – Any organizational change that improves on previously established processes and procedures.
2. Transitional change – Change that moves an organization away from its current state to a new state in order to solve a problem, such as mergers and acquisitions and automation.
3. Transformational change – Change that radically and fundamentally alters the culture and operation of an organization. In transformational change, the end result may not be known. For example, a company may pursue entirely different products or markets.

As a conceptual business framework for people, processes, and the organization, change management increases the success of critical projects and initiatives and improves a company's ability to adapt quickly.

13.3 Communication

Lean thinking is fundamentally transforming the way organizations operate. The lean principles of continuous improvement, respect for people, and a relentless focus on delivering customer value are making teams and organizations rethink the practices that might have guided them for decades. The introduction of lean production requires in parallel a lean communication process. Communication is an important aspect of lean process in order to successfully implement lean processes or activities.

13.4 Empowerment and Bottom-Up Culture

Taking workers' opinions and proposals into account, valuing their proposals to motivate them, implementing proposals, or, should they not be applicable, explaining why. Change in management behaviour: communication, transparency, and contact with the shop floor, less information flow stagnation, and continuous management support along with greater accountability to workers.

13.5 Job Design

The job design is about the design how and where tasks are performed by employees. Most work is complex enough that it is subdivided into tasks performed at different stages, so that different people and/or departments must interact with each other to complete the work. Work design is about the coordination of these interactions creating an organization. Lean is about achieving operational excellence. Therefore, the first step towards a lean work design is to create a work design that allows individuals within the system to achieve operational excellence. The job design includes (1) the job description, (2) the physical environment in which the tasks are executed, and the (3) management which must provide the necessary framework and tools to do the job.

13.6 Shopfloor Management (SFM)

One of the most important differences between traditional manufacturing systems and lean systems centres on the behaviours and roles employees are expected to adopt. Unlike conventional hierarchical command-and-control structures, lean HR policies and practices reinforce employee empowerment. Employees from shopfloor to management are encouraged to engage in continuous improvement activities aimed at eliminating waste (suggestion schemes, quality circles) and to get involved in the proactive aspects of production (problem-solving, target-setting, decision-making). To develop employee appreciation for the manufacturing process and customer value, multi-skilling, job rotation, and cross-functional teamworking are encouraged. Since its advert, lean has transformed the manufacturing world, demonstrating a remarkable ability to improve the quality, productivity, and lead times of manufacturing companies in many different industry sectors (Liker 2004). It currently represents, as Ohno (1990) outlined, the standard manufacturing approach of the twenty-first century with as many as 50 percent of UK-owned and 85 percent of US-owned firms applying lean techniques in at least part of their business.

13.7 Motivation as a Key Success Factor in Lean Management

The Toyota Production System or lean management has been described in many ways. It is the systematic elimination of waste. It is continuous improvement. It is striving for interruption-free processes. It is a passionate focus on serving customers. It is many things. But one aspect of lean that has not been given enough attention, in my opinion, is how lean is an organization wide system of motivation that creates a high-performance culture (Helmold and Samara 2019). The Toyota Production System or lean management has been described in many ways. It is the systematic elimination of waste. It is continuous improvement. It is striving for interruption-free processes. It is a passionate focus on serving customers. It is many things. But one aspect of lean that has not been given enough attention, in my opinion, is how lean is an organization-wide system of motivation that creates a high-performance culture.

Too many lean implementations suffer from a focus on problem-solving skills, but a failure to attend to the system or culture of motivation. Too many rely on the "they oughtta wanna" assumption, which usually results in disappointment.

Ultimately all organization performance comes down to human behaviour, and there are always two aspects to achieving high performance: one is competence and the other is motivation. There must be competence in technical skills, and there must be competence in social skills such as teamwork and problem-solving, for example. Skills are useless unless individuals are motivated to use them. From my experience at Toyota and Honda and other high-performing organizations, there is a high degree of motivation for not only personal success but the collective success of the group – the team and the company. Many of those implementing lean would do well to focus more on creating a systematic approach to motivating all members of the organization.

13.8 Case Study: Tesla's Lean Transformation

In the case of Tesla, the company imposes various techniques and measurement to keep track of the company's performance, which is primarily based on productivity. For example, the company measures its manufacturing performance based on the number of cars produced a day; for the customer service division, it considers the number of inquiries resolved, emails answered, and complaints handled. In addition, Tesla also establishes key performance indicators (KPI) to monitor its production and inventory and generally assess the success of achieving the goals within the predetermined duration. In fact, for prospective managers at Tesla Inc., familiarity and experience with applying and monitoring KPIs for a particular area are not just huge advantages but also part of job responsibilities.

Tesla's key stakeholders include its investors, directors, employees, suppliers, shareholders, partners, the government, financial institutes, and the public. Communicating performance to these entities is not limited to disclosing the company's financial reports but also informs them about the company's visions, strategies, targets, milestones, key issues, and major accomplishments.

Tesla Motors Inc. has maintained regular and efficient communication with its stakeholders. The company publishes its annual report on its website, disclosing key financial data, the company's strengths and values, potential risk factors, its products, services, network and infrastructures, and other important information (Tesla 2016). The company also communicates with its stakeholders by organizing annual meetings for its stockholders with webcasts for those who cannot attend in person, Q&A conference calls to share the company's quarterly financial results, and factory tours for those who want to have a closer look at the company's manufacturing and operations (Tesla 2016). The company also manages its own blogs and official pages on social media websites including Facebook and Twitter to keep stakeholders abreast of the company's latest developments and achievements.

In case some major crisis happens, the company also responds very promptly to keep the crisis under control. For example, when a video showing a Tesla Model S catching fire went viral on YouTube in 2013, Elon Musk, Tesla's CEO, quickly shared a post on the company's blog to explain the reasons behind the accident, regain customers' trust in Tesla's vehicles, and reaffirm the company's potentials with the investors (Russolillo and Cheng, 2013).

Tesla aims at mass producing electric cars and make them as ubiquitous as gasoline-powered cars. To do that, they have to produce affordable cars and meet the huge demand the promise of pollution-free transportation is generating in the market.

The launch of the mass market Tesla Model 3 has been dogged by production problems with the number of unfulfilled orders exceeding the ability of the company to deliver. Tesla's CEO Elon Musk has talked about been in a "production hell" – working tirelessly to get production moving at the right pace.

In the past 1 year or so, Elon Musk has transformed his idea of what is required to meet production targets. He has gone from thinking that excessive automation is the answer to his productivity challenges to recently admitting that there are areas that are best left to manual human labour. In this interview, Elon even showed more admiration for low tech "dumb robots" that use simple sensors and magnetic strips to move material to various workstations within the factory.

This transformation has taken some time to come, and – as a member of the lean community – it is gratifying to witness it.

Manual labour is better than robots especially when they are complicated as they will require specialized and expensive engineering expertise. In an factory operation that runs continuously for 24 hours, this means that these technicians will have to be available all the time in case of breakdowns. This extra layer of highly paid support labour will increase the operating costs and eat into the company's profits.

The fact that the robots are specialized for specific tasks within the factory means that there is a lot of downtime when they breakdown.

The removal of conveyors – which Musk said ended up complicating things even more – is another indication that lean manufacturing principles are taking root at Tesla.

Conveyors added a level of complexity that led to lower productivity. The conveyors – which were later removed – needed constant attention from engineers so that they do not break down. Removing things that do not add value is a major activity when doing lean manufacturing.

Another thing, conveyors tend to move material very fast. This may sound like a good thing, but it may actually be the cause a significant drop in productivity. Why is this? Conveyors that transport material faster than the speed of the line end up creating bottlenecks because of build-up of work in process. Resources are required to handle this material build-up, and this leads to more manpower being deployed – hence the low productivity.

The Tesla factory processes are arranged in a U shape. This type of layout is very efficient in the utilization of space and also gives visibility to what is happening on the line. The logic is simple – a straight line layout will require more space lengthwise. Bending the line in a U shape can save up to 50 percent of the space required by the assembly line.

Another advantage a u-shape line has over a line layout is that the input and output sections are next to each other. This makes designing of receiving and shipping bay much easier.

Set-up times for machines and processes are lower in U-shaped lines. Another advantage is that sharing of equipment for different product line becomes much easier – thereby saving capital cost on duplicate machines.

It is a good thing that Tesla is starting to use the time-tested lean manufacturing principles in its production process. They will have to continue experimenting on the best way to bring about their vision of a mass produced affordable electric car. Getting there will require a dogged determination to succeed as well as the humility to accept counsel from people who have done it better.

Above all, embracing lean manufacturing means that you have to take everyone on board and unleash the creativity of your workforce to solve problems.

Tesla should replace its top-down management style with a bottom-up approach that takes input from lower cadres so as to improve productivity, quality, and profitability.

References

Helmold, M., & Samara, W. (2019). *Progress in performance management. Industry insights and case studies on principles, application tools, and practice*. Heidelberg: Springer.

Helmold, M., & Terry, B. (2016). *Global sourcing and supply management excellence in China. Procurement guide for supply experts*. Singapore: Springer.

Kalkis, H., Roja, Z., & Babris, S. (2019). Human factor and LEAN analysis at industrial manufacturing plants. In J. Kantola, S. Nazir, & T. Barath (Eds.), *Advances in human factors, business management and society. AHFE 2018. Advances in intelligent systems and computing, vol 783*. Wiesbaden: Springer.

Liker, J. K. (2004). *The Toyota way*. Madison: McGraw-Hill.

Ohno, T. (1990). *Toyota production system. Beyond large scale production*. New York: Productivity Press.

Russolillo, S., & Cheng, J. (2013). Day Traders Steer Tesla Higher. In: Wallstreet Journal. Retrieved 11.5.2020. https://www.wsj.com/articles/SB10001424127887323398204578487522937316796.

Tesla (2016). www.tesla.com.

Lean Management and Artificial Intelligence (AI)

14

Now the playbook is we build AI tools to go find these fake accounts, find coordinated networks of inauthentic activity, and take them down; we make it much harder for anyone to advertise in ways that they shouldn't be.

Marc Zuckerberg (1984-today)

14.1 Industry 4.0 in Lean Management

Production systems are not like they used to be. The twenty-first century will confront enterprises and manufacturing companies with completely novel generations of technologies, services, and products based on computer technologies (Schuh and Gottschalk 2008). In order to meet competition on global markets and to ensure long-term success, the companies need to adapt to shorter delivery times, increasing product variability and high market volatility, by which enterprises are able to sensitively and timely react to continuous and unexpected changes (Wiendahl et al. 2007). One of the major cornerstones to meet these challenges is the implementation of digital information and communication technologies into production systems, processes, and technologies, which allow novel developments by combining the physical world and fast data access and data processing via the Internet (Industry 4.0).

Industry 4.0 is a name given to the current trend of automation and data exchange in manufacturing technologies. It includes cyber-physical systems, the Internet of Things, cloud computing, and cognitive computing. Industry 4.0 is commonly referred to as the fourth industrial revolution. Industry 4.0 fosters what has been called a "smart factory". Within modular structured smart factories, cyber-physical systems monitor physical processes create a virtual copy of the physical world and make decentralized decisions. Over the Internet of Things, cyber-physical systems

M. Helmold, *Lean Management and Kaizen*, Management for Professionals,
https://doi.org/10.1007/978-3-030-46981-8_14

communicate and cooperate with each other and with humans in real-time both internally and across organizational services offered and used by participants of the value chain. There are four design principles in Industry 4.0. These principles support companies in identifying and implementing Industry 4.0 scenarios (Helmold and Samara 2019) Fig. 14.1:

- Interconnection: The ability of machines, devices, sensors, and people to connect and communicate with each other via the Internet of Things (IoT) or the Internet of People (IoP).
- Information transparency: The transparency afforded by Industry 4.0 technology provides operators with vast amounts of useful information needed to make appropriate decisions. Interconnectivity allows operators to collect immense amounts of data and information from all points in the manufacturing process, thus aiding functionality and identifying key areas that can benefit from innovation and improvement.
- Technical assistance: First, the ability of assistance systems to support humans by aggregating and visualizing information comprehensively for making informed decisions and solving urgent problems on short notice. Second, the ability of cyber-physical systems to physically support humans by conducting a range of tasks that are unpleasant, too exhausting, or unsafe for their human co-workers
- Decentralized decisions: The ability of cyber-physical systems to make decisions on their own and to perform their tasks as autonomously as possible. Only in the case of exceptions, interferences, or conflicting goals are tasks delegated to a higher level

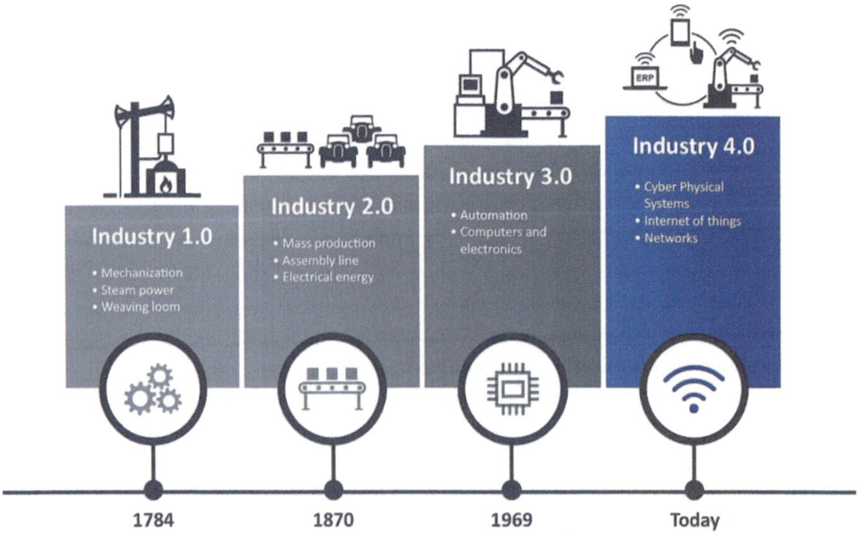

Fig. 14.1 Industry 4.0 Evolution. (Source: Adopted from Industry 4.0: The Top 9 Trends For 2018 (Liubomyr (El.) Kachur))

14.2 Artificial Intelligence (AI) in Lean Management

14.2.1 Lean AI Tools Will Lead to a Competitive Advantage

In the field of computer science, artificial intelligence (AI), sometimes called machine intelligence, is intelligence demonstrated by machines, in contrast to the natural intelligence displayed by humans and other animals. Figure 14.2 depicts nine lean elements of artificial intelligence which can be lead to a competitive advantage across the value chain (Helmold and Samara 2019).

14.2.2 Autonomous Robots

An autonomous robot is a robot that performs behaviours or tasks with a high degree of autonomy (without external influence). Autonomous robotics is usually considered to be a subfield of artificial intelligence, robotics, and information engineering.

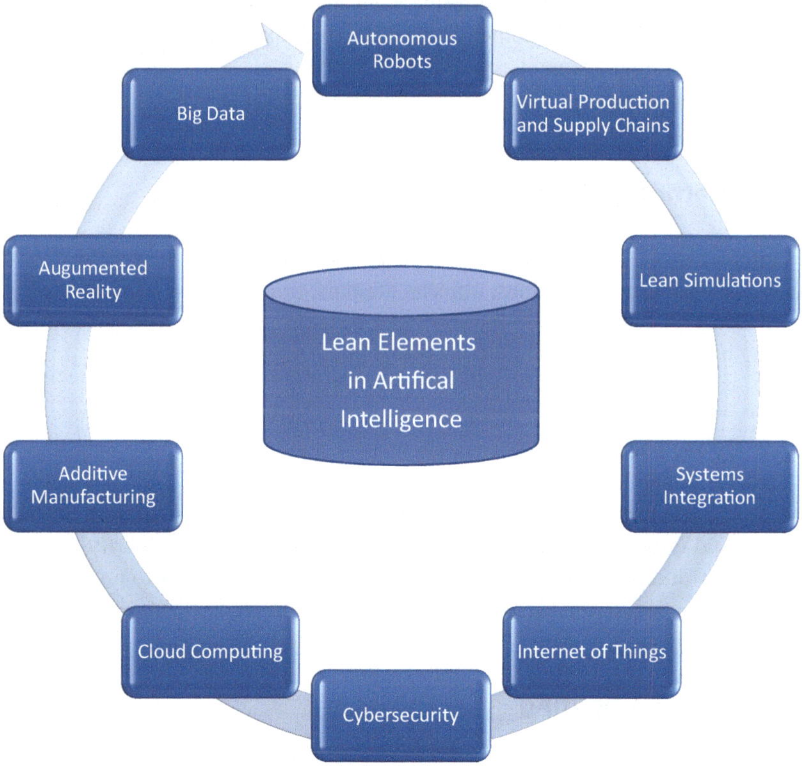

Fig. 14.2 Trends in AI. (Source: Author's Source)

14.2.3 Virtual Production and Supply Chains

Virtual production tends to be used to help visualize complex scenes or scenes that simply cannot be filmed for real. In general, though, virtual production can really refer to any techniques that allow filmmakers to plan, imagine, or complete some kind of filmic element, typically with the aid of digital tools.

14.2.4 Lean Simulations

Lean simulations include a set of hands-on experiments to teach employees about systems and process improvement in all areas of the value chain. Lean simulations can focus on design, manufacturing, capacity planning, or supply chain design. Purposes of simulations are to understand the implications of input variables and alternations of the value chain elements.

14.2.5 System Integration

Lean integration is a continuous improvement methodology for bringing disparate data and software systems together. The goal is to maximize customer value. Lean integration is a management system that emphasizes eliminating waste as a sustainable data integration and system integration practice.

14.2.6 Internet of Things

The Internet of Things (IoT) is a system of interrelated computing devices, mechanical and digital machines, objects, animals, or people that are provided with unique identifiers (UIDs) and the ability to transfer data over a network without requiring human-to-human or human-to-computer interaction.

14.2.7 Cybersecurity

Cybersecurity is the protection of internet-connected systems, including hardware, software, and data, from cyberattacks. In a computing context, security comprises cybersecurity and physical security – both are used by enterprises to protect against unauthorized access to data centres and other computerized systems.

14.2.8 Cloud Computing

Cloud computing is a type of computing that relies on shared computing resources rather than having local servers or personal devices to handle applications. In its most simple description, cloud computing is taking services ("cloud services") and moving them outside an organization's IT system and environment.

14.2.9 Additive Manufacturing

Additive manufacturing (AM) is the industrial production name for 3D printing, a computer-controlled process that creates three-dimensional objects by depositing materials, usually in layers. The official industry standard term is the ASTM F2792 for all applications of the 3D technology. It is defined as the process of joining materials to make objects from 3D model data, usually layer upon layer, as opposed to subtractive *manufacturing* methodologies.

14.2.10 Augmented Reality

Augmented reality (AR) is an interactive experience of a real-world environment where the objects that reside in the real world are enhanced by computer-generated perceptual information, sometimes across multiple sensory modalities, including visual, auditory, haptic, somatosensory, and olfactory.

14.2.11 Big Data

Big Data is a phrase used to mean a massive volume of both structured and unstructured data that is so large it is difficult to process using traditional database and software techniques. In most enterprise scenarios, the volume of data is too big or it moves too fast or it exceeds current processing capacity.

14.3 Case Study: Google's Self-Driving Cars

Research into self-driving cars is not a new phenomenon. In the late 1950s, the first known thoughts on self-driving vehicles were described in *Popular Mechanics* magazine by a mechanic who argued that altering a roadster to both start itself and back itself into a driveway would be relatively straightforward. Later that year, a GM analyst revealed in *Popular Science* magazine that the company was already investigating embedding highways with cable and radio-control boxes as a means of developing an infrastructure to support driverless cars. Despite all of the theoretical research into the subject, self-driving cars did not become a reality until 1968. The first physical breakthrough in driverless car technology was the design of a car that used sonar and gyroscopes to drive, steer, and stop an automobile. In 1968, The Cornell Aeronautical Laboratory created the "Urbmobile", an electric car that could be driven on the road but could also glide along a subway-style track that utilized roadside guides, magnetometers, magnetic nails, and internal computers. The largest breakthrough came years later, however, with the announcement from Google, Inc. of the Google Car in 2010. With the distinctive sensor and camera nub lodged on top of a Toyota Prius, the Google Car quickly became operational and present on roads across the USA. Shortly thereafter, media coverage of the Google Car became increasingly prevalent in addition to promotional commercials demonstrating the benefits of the car (Google 2019). While the benefits demonstrated in the videos seemed to be promising, the Google Car's entrance into the market seemed a far leap away from Google's core business. Google Inc. specializes in Internet-related services and products, with the mission to organize the world's information and make it universally accessible and useful. In 1998, Larry Page and Sergey Brin, two Stanford University computer science graduate students, created a search engine that uses back links, or incoming links, to a website or web page, to determine the importance and therefore rank individual web pages during a web query. Existing competitors, like Yahoo and AOL, on the other hand, were directories of other websites, organized in a hierarchy, as opposed to a searchable index of pages. This allows the Google search process to return more relevant results rather than simply a ranked list of preferred sites. In 1999, Google secured funding from Sequoia Capital and Kleiner Perkins Caufield & Byers, Silicon Valley's two leading venture capital firms (Google 2019). Only 1 year later, Google became the world's largest search engine with over a billion pages in its index, surpassing industry giants such as Yahoo. Google's dominance of the search market continues today as Google maintains a 67 percent share of global searches. While Google Inc. began as a company specializing in search, it quickly expanded into other product areas. In 2004, Google launched Gmail, an email client which became the world's largest email provider by 2012 with an estimated 425 million active users. Expanding into the online video domain, Google acquired YouTube in 2006 for $1.65 billion, which reaches over 1 billion unique visitors each month. In 2008, Google launched Chrome, a web browser, and Android, an operating system for mobile devices. In both of these areas as well, Google dominates the market, with a 50 percent and 68 percent of the market share, respectively (Miller and Wald 2013). In 2010, Google announced that the prototype of a driverless car – the Google Car – was completed (Google 2019). According to Google executives at the time, the goal of the Google Car was to "... help prevent traffic accidents, free up people's time and reduce carbon emissions by fundamentally changing car use". With a team assembled consisting of engineers with experience in vehicle technology from the DARPA Challenges, a series of driverless vehicle races sponsored by the US Government, Google was finally able to bring the driverless car phenomenon to reality. The Google Car is a sophisticated system that integrates proprietary hardware and software, using video cameras, radar sensors, and a laser range finder to visualize traffic and detailed maps taken from Google Maps to enable navigation between destinations. Google's data centres process the incoming data relayed from the sensors and cameras mounted on the Google Car in order to provide the car with useful information about its environment that is later translated into the physical operation of the vehicle. The key to the Google Car's technological capabilities is the laser range finder mounted on the roof of the modified Toyota Prius, allowing for real-time environmental analysis. In addition, the Google Car is equipped with four radars and a velodyne 64-beam laser placed strategically around the car to accurately generate a three-dimensional map of its environment. A camera detects traffic lights, while a GPS, wheel encoder, and inertial measurement unit control the vehicle's location and logs car movement. The software system synthesizes laser measurements produced from the laser beam with high-resolution maps of the world, producing dynamic data models then translated into the physical operation of the vehicle by the car's internal software system. Altogether, the system allows for seamless operation of the vehicle that adjusts to its dynamic environment without the intervention of a driver. In addition to the generic driverless capability, the Google Car's system also adjusts for local traffic laws and environmental obstacles in real time. For example, if the Google Car approaches a four-way intersection and senses that the driver with the right of way does not move, the Google Car inches forward slightly to indicate to other drivers the intentions of driving through the intersection (Miller and Wald 2013).

Altogether, the technology and adaptation to local conditions not only allows for driverless transportation but also increases safety on the road. Since its introduction, the Google Car has completed 200,000 miles of accident-free computer-led driving, beyond one incident that was arguably caused by another driver. The road test results for the Google Car indicate that the Google Car obeys all of the rules of the road and adjusts to its dynamic environment in real-time with no problems. Thus, with this integrated technology, the car has the capability of being safer than a human driver. The Google Car has the potential to have a profound effect on energy consumption, efficiency, and traffic accidents. With subsequent productivity increases, and decreases in costs, the Google Car represents a potentially revolutionizing technology. It is precisely this potential, however, that creates a threat for Google to sustaining a long-term competitive advantage in the driverless car space. As the Google Car may radically shift the structure of affected industries and raises serious privacy concerns, vulnerable industries and consumer groups threaten the viability of the project. Thus, the Google Car faces challenges far greater than competing car manufacturers alone. In squaring off against politically and economically powerful industries that are facing their demise, can the Google Car survive? Can the will to revolutionize driving outweigh the costs of potentially ruined industries and massive unemployment? Who will win the war of the road?

References

Google. (2019). www.google.com

Helmold, M., & Samara, W. (2019). *Progress in performance management. Industry insights and case studies on principles, application tools, and practice*. Heidelberg: Springer.

Miller, C. C., & Wald, M. L. (2013). Self-driving cars for testing are supported by U.S. *New York Times*. Retrieved 10.12.2019. https://www.nytimes.com/2013/05/31/technology/self-driving-cars-for-testing-are-supported-by-us.html.

Schuh, G., & Gottschalk, S. (2008). Product Engineering. Production engineering for self-organizing complex systems. In: Production Engineering, 2. Jg., 2008, Nr. 4, S. 43431–435.

Wiendahl, H.-P. et al. (2007). Changeable Manufacturing. Classification, Design and Operations. International Institution for Production Engineering Research. S.1–25.

15 Sustainability and Lean Management

It takes 20 years to build a reputation and five minutes to ruin it.

Benjamin Franklin (1706–1790)

15.1 CSR and Lean Management

Corporate social responsibility (CSR) is also known by a number of other names. These include corporate responsibility, corporate accountability, corporate ethics, corporate citizenship or stewardship, business ethics, responsible entrepreneurship, and triple bottom line, to name just a few. As CSR issues become increasingly integrated into modern business practices, there is a trend towards referring to it as "responsible competitiveness" or "corporate sustainability". CSR is understood to be the way firms integrate social, environmental, and economic concerns into their values, culture, decision-making, strategy, and operations in a transparent and accountable manner and thereby establish better practices within the firm, create wealth, and improve society. A key point to note is that CSR is an evolving concept that currently does not have a universally accepted definition. Generally, CSR is understood to be the way firms integrate social, environmental, and economic concerns into their values, culture, decision-making, strategy, and operations in a transparent and accountable manner and thereby establish better practices within the firm, create wealth, and improve society. As issues of sustainable development become more important, the question of how the business sector addresses them is also becoming an element of CSR. The World Business Council for Sustainable Development has described CSR as the business contribution to sustainable economic development. Building on a base of compliance with legislation and regulations, CSR typically includes "beyond law" commitments and activities pertaining to:

M. Helmold, *Lean Management and Kaizen*, Management for Professionals,
https://doi.org/10.1007/978-3-030-46981-8_15

- Corporate governance and ethics
- Health and safety
- Environmental stewardship
- Human rights (including core labour rights)
- Sustainable development
- Conditions of work (including safety and health, hours of work, wages)
- Industrial relations
- Community involvement, development, and investment
- Involvement of and respect for diverse cultures and disadvantaged peoples
- Corporate philanthropy and employee volunteering
- Customer satisfaction and adherence to principles of fair competitio
- Anti-bribery and anti-corruption measures
- Accountability, transparency, and performance reporting
- Supplier relations, for both domestic and international supply chains

Lean manufacturing concepts focus primarily on improvements of the operational processes and efficiency. Another goal is to reduce waste and thus to reduce operating costs. In the last years sustainability has become more and more important, so that any organization must deploy sustainability elements alongside a lean organization. Sustainability or corporate social responsibility (CSR) has the following elements as shown in Fig. 15.1. The figure shows that there is a strong need to align the lean implementation process with the sustainability strategy in order to avoid the negative impacts that lean production could have on the environmental and social components of sustainability. Although the concept of corporate social responsibility (CSR) has been advocated for decades and is commonly employed by corporations globally, agreement on how CSR should be defined and implemented remains a contentious debate among academia, businesses, and society. This gap is problematic for corporations because they are increasingly being required to align with societal norms while generating financial returns. In order to remedy this problem, the following definition is presented: corporate social responsibility is a business system that enables the production and distribution of wealth for the betterment of its stakeholders through the implementation and integration of ethical systems and sustainable management practices. Many of the concepts in the proposed definition are commonplace among CSR practitioners and organizations; the validations for the key segments – production and distribution of wealth, stakeholder

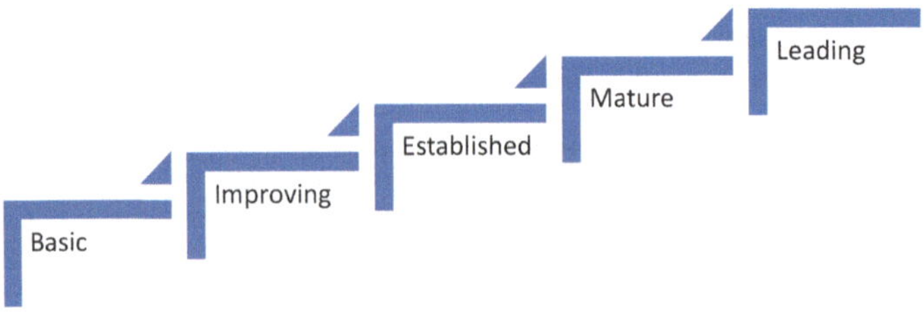

Fig. 15.1 CSR Maturity Levels. (Helmold and Samara 2019)

management, ethical systems, and sustainable management practices – coupled with the application of a systems approach and other business practices make the definition unique and conclusive.

15.2 CSR Maturity Levels

Maturity is a measurement of the ability of an organization for continuous improvement in CSR as shown in Fig. 15.1. The higher the maturity, the higher will be the chances that incidents or errors will lead to improvements either in the quality or in the use of the resources of the discipline as implemented by the organization.

15.3 Global Compact Principles

Corporate sustainability starts with a company's value system and a principles-based approach to doing business. This means operating in ways that, at a minimum, meet fundamental responsibilities in the areas of human rights, labour, environment, and anti-corruption. Responsible businesses enact the same values and principles wherever they have a presence and know that good practices in one area do not offset harm in another. By incorporating the Ten Principles of the UN Global Compact into strategies, policies, and procedures, and establishing a culture of integrity, companies are not only upholding their basic responsibilities to people and planet but also setting the stage for long-term success. The UN Global Compact is a principle-based framework for businesses, stating ten principles in the areas of human rights, labour, the environment, and anti-corruption. Under the Global Compact, companies are brought together with UN agencies, labour groups, and civil society. The framework provides a universal language for corporate responsibility and a framework to guide all businesses regardless of size, complexity, or location. Joining the UN Global Compact means to take an important public step to transform our world through principled business. Participation makes a statement about values, and it benefits both society and companies' long-term success.

Corporate sustainability starts with a company's value system and a principled approach to doing business. This means operating in ways that, at a minimum, meet fundamental responsibilities in the areas of human rights, labour, environment, and anti-corruption. Responsible businesses enact the same values and principles wherever they have a presence and know that good practices in one area do not offset harm in another. By incorporating the Global Compact principles into strategies, policies, and procedures, and establishing a culture of integrity, companies are not only upholding their basic responsibilities to people and planet but also setting the stage for long-term success (Fig. 15.2).

10 Principles of the UN Global Compact

Human Rights	Principle 1: Businesses should support and respect internationally proclaimed human rights; and Principle 2: ensure that they are not complicit in human rights abuses.
Labour	Principle 3: Businesses should uphold the freedom of association and recognize effectively the right to collective bargaining; Principle 4: eliminate all forms of forced and compulsory labour; Principle 5: effectively abolish child labour; and Principle 6: eliminate discrimination in respect of employment and occupation.
Environment	Principle 7: Businesses should support a precautionary approach to environmental challenges; Principle 8: undertake initiatives to promote greater environmental responsibility; and Principle 9: encourage the development and diffusion of environmentally friendly technologies.
Anti-Corruption	Principle 10: Businesses should work against corruption in all its forms, including extortion and bribery.

Fig. 15.2 Global Compact Principles. (Source: United Nations)

15.4 Case Study: Volkswagen's Lean and Green Award

The Volkswagen Wolfsburg plant receives the "Lean & Green Management Award 2019" in the "Automotive OEM" category for its efficient and sustainable production. More than 250 works from more than 10 countries and 20 different industries participated in the competition. "We are proud that our persistent work has been successful in saving resources and that we have been awarded the prestigious 'Lean & Green Management Award' for this," said Stefan Loth, Head of Volkswagen's Wolfsburg plant. "At the Wolfsburg location, we prove that efficient vehicle production while at the same time conserving resources is not only possible, but makes sense. Because the production also carries an ecological responsibility. The deliberate use of raw materials and energy plays a key role in our environmental commitment." In terms of production efficiency, Volkswagen's parent plant focuses on its 'PQM' strategy - productivity, quality and crew. Every year more than 400 workshops take place, with which the Wolfsburg workforce improves the processes and thus reduces the production costs per vehicle. The plant consistently uses the Volkswagen Production system that describes the basics, standards and methods by which the manufacturing processes are designed, executed and constantly developed. The Volkswagen parent plant is also on course for sustainability and the implementation of the "Zero Impact Factory" environmental program. An important building block for protecting the environment and promoting biodiversity are,

Fig. 15.3 Volkswagen Lean and Green Award 2019. (Source: Volkswagen)

for example, the process water basins located on the plant site. Thanks to the internal operating water cycle, every drop of water passes through the site about four to six times, helping to keep water consumption per vehicle very low. The "Lean & Green Management Award" is awarded annually by the consultants Growtth Consulting Europe and Quadriga Consult and the trade publication AUTOMOBIL INDUSTRIE. The award was recently ranked as one of the highest rated sustainability awards in Germany in a study by the University of Hohenheim (Fig. 15.3).

Reference

Helmold, M., & Samara, W. (2019). *Progress in performance management. Industry insights and case studies on principles, application tools, and practice*. Heidelberg: Springer.

Lean Management in the Service Industry 16

Get closer than ever to your customers. So close that you tell them what they need well before they realize it themselves.

Steve Jobs.

16.1 Importance of Service Sector

The term "service sector" refers to an economic sector that, unlike agriculture and industry, produces no goods, but provides a service that satisfies a need. Education, health, finance, government, transportation, and trade are service sectors. The statistics show the gross value-added in Germany in the years from 1991 to 2018 by economic sector. The gross value-added in the service sectors in 2018 was around 2068.18 billion euros (Rudnika 2018).

The service industry is the largest and fastest-growing business sector in Germany. In 2017, about 69 percent of total value-added was generated in the service sectors. In particular, the field of "public service providers, education, health" contributes the most to the gross value-added. Overall, the area reached more than 536 billion euros in 2017. Other important service sectors are "Trade, Hospitality and Transport" with around € 474 billion, "Business Service Providers" with around € 324 billion, and "Land and Housing" with € 317.5 billion. The majority of taxable businesses in the service sector in Germany exist in the areas of "trade, maintenance and repair of motor vehicles" with around 604,400 and the "provision of professional, scientific and technical services", which includes, inter alia, tax advice and auditing. Services are different from products and have the characteristics as shown in Fig. 16.1:

M. Helmold, *Lean Management and Kaizen*, Management for Professionals, https://doi.org/10.1007/978-3-030-46981-8_16

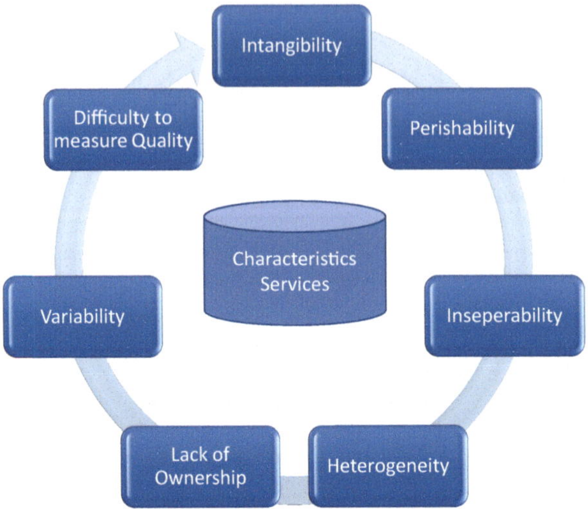

Fig. 16.1 Characteristics of services. (Source: Author's Source)

16.2 Intangibility

Intangibility is an important consideration that complicates the functional responsibility of a marketing manager, especially while influencing and motivating the prospects/customers. The goods of tangible nature can be displayed, the prospects or buyers can have a view, and they can even test and make a trial before making the buying decisions. The selling processes are thus found easier. We are aware of the fact that services are of intangible nature and it is intangibility that complicates the task of decision-makers.

While motivating, they find it difficult to perform and display, and the positive or negative opinions regarding the services come up only after the completion of the using process. The customer can't touch the services; they albeit can't smell them. In a true sense, it is not a physical object. It has mental connotations. According to Carman and Uhl, a buyer of products (goods) has an opportunity to see, touch, hear, smell, or taste them before they buy.

Of course, we don't find the same thing with the services product. It is the professional excellence of decision-makers that counts here that influences the entire process and that helps them substantially. While selling or promoting services, we need to concentrate on benefits and satisfaction which a buyer can derive after buying. We can hardly emphasize the service itself.

As, for example, the banking organizations promote the sale of credit cards by visualizing the conveniences and comforts the holders of the credit cards are likely to get from the same. Services carry with them a combination of intangible perceptions. As, for instance, an airline sells the seat from one destination to another.

Here, it is a matter of consumers' perception of the services and their expectations not smelling or tasting the services. They expect safe, fast, decent services. A service by nature is an abstract phenomenon. Thus, it is right to mention that due to intangibility, the selling and marketing of services become much more complicated.

16.3 Perishability

Another point complicating the task of a professional is the nature of perishability that we find in the services. The goods if not sold today can be stored, preserved for further selling. Thus, the risk element is here in a different form. But in the context of services, if we fail to sell the services, it is lost only not for today but even for the future. If a labour stops to work, if a seat in the aircraft remains unsold, if a bedroom in a hotel remains unbooked, if a chair in a cinema hall remains vacant, we find the business non-existent, and the opportunities are lost and lost forever. The services can't be stored or preserved. Unutilized or underutilized services are found to be a waste. A building unoccupied, a person unemployed, credit unutilized, and vacant beds in a hospital are economic waste. Of course, this is due mainly to its perishability. This makes it essential that decision-makers or the executives by using their professionalism minimize the possibilities of economic waste. The opportunities come and you need to capitalize on the same by using your excellence.

16.4 Inseparability

This is also a feature that complicates the task of professionals while marketing the services. The inseparability focuses on the fact that the services are not of separable nature. Generally, the services are created and supplied simultaneously. Like the dancers, musicians, dentists, and other professionals create and offer services at the same time. In other words, the services and their providers are the same. Donald Cowell says, "Goods are produced, sold and then consumed whereas the services are sold and then produced and consumed".

It is inseparability that makes the task of marketing services a bit difficult. The goods are produced at one point and then distributed by others at other points. In the services, we find the selling processes making ways for the generation of services. The professionals while marketing the services thus bear the responsibility of removing or minimizing the gap between the services-promised and services-offered.

Goods are produced, sold, and then consumed but the services are sold, produced, and then used. The inseparability thus makes it essential that the service providers are acting and behaving professionally so that the marketing processes are not to pave the avenues for a degeneration in the quality.

16.5 Heterogeneity

Another feature is heterogeneity which makes it difficult to establish standard. The quality of services can't be standardized. The prices charged may be too high or too low. In the case of entertainment and sports, we find the same thing. The same type of services can't be sold to all the customers even if they pay the same price.

The consumers rate the services in a different way. Of course, it is due to the difference in the perception of individuals at the levels of providers and users. The heterogeneity factor makes it difficult to market efficiently. The professionals by using their excellence bear the responsibility of minimizing the problem.

16.6 Lack of Ownership

It is also ownership that makes it significant to market the services in a bit different way. The goods sold are transferred from one place to another, the ownership is also transferred, and this provides to the buyers an opportunity to resell. In the case of services, we don't find the same thing. The users have just an access to the service. As, for example, a consumer can use personal care services or Medicare services or can use a hotel room or swimming pool; however the ownership rests with the providers. An expert opines, "A service is any activity or benefit that one party can offer to another that it is essentially intangible and does not result in the ownership of anything". Here, it is clear that ownership is not affected in the process of selling the services. The issue of ownership has also been clarified by another expert. He says, "Services are those separately identifiable, essentially intangible activities which provide want satisfaction and that are not necessarily tied to use sales of a product or another services. To produce a service may or may not require the use of tangible goods. However, when such use is required, there is no transfer of permanent ownership to these tangible goods". The same theme of not transferring the ownership has also been supported by Batesan. Here, the focus is on the point that transfer of ownership simplifies the task of a marketer since he/she can use it as a motivational tool. In case of services, the professionals experience difficulties because we don't find any scope for the transfer of ownership. The professionals thus need to be more careful while selling or marketing the services.

16.7 Variability

Physical goods are produced with a high degree of standardization. They are factory produced or assembled in large numbers with enormous consistency. It is rare to find two cakes of soap like Pears or two pieces of car like Alto different from one another. However, this kind of similarity is near impossible in services. For instance, two visits to a doctor or two lectures of a professor are never exactly same. Two separate stays at a particular hotel are unlikely to be an exact replica of one another. Variability is inherent in services because of their peculiar characteristics including intangibility and inseparability.

There are several reasons that make standardization of services difficult. First, intangibility prevents setting up of precisely defined standards for service product, their conformance, and control. The advances in quality like zero defect has been possible due to their tangible character.

Physical goods have tangible dimensions that permit setting up of quality standards, deviations measurement, and their minimization. Second, service variability is caused by human involvement and customer-provider interactions. Services are produced and consumed in real time.

Unlike goods, services cannot be produced and then quality checked. The lack of separation between production and consumption prevents post-production quality control. A major difference between product marketing and service marketing is that one cannot control the quality of service results, whereas the quality control engineer on a production line can control the quality of his product at any time.

When you buy a box of Tide, you can be sure that it will work to get your clothes clean. When you buy a Holiday Inn room, you are sure to some lesser percentage that it will work to give a good night's sleep without any hassle, or people banging on walls and all the bad things that can happen to you in a hotel'. Each service episode tends to be unique in its own right. The interaction between customer and provider cannot be programmed and controlled cent per cent. In spite of a highly regimented service delivery process, each customer brings unique psycho-social aspect to a service encounter. For instance, service encounters are affected by moods and personality combinations between provider and customer. For instance, service provider's mood and emotional state despite high training is difficult to control like a machine. Similarly, one customer is unlikely to have similar mental state in two service episodes. Service inconsistency manifests in different forms. For instance, quality variation can be experienced across different service outlets, for example, two branches of Cafe Coffee Day (CCD) may provide different service experience (Helmold and Terry 2016). Variations in service can also be found across time too. For instance, the service quality between lunch and dinner services of a restaurant may differ.

16.8 Difficulty to Measure Quality of Services

The quality of service requires another tool for measurement. We can't measure it in terms of service level. It is very difficult to rate or quantify the total purchase. As, for example, we can quantify the food served in a hotel, but the way a waiter or a carrier serves it or overall environment or behaviour of other staff can't be ignored while rating the total process (Helmold and Samara 2019). Hence, we can determine the level of satisfaction at which the users are found satisfied. A firm sells atmosphere, conveniences, consistent quality, status, anxiety, moral, etc.

16.9 Lean Management Principles in Service Sector

Companies in the service sector are constantly under pressure to deliver excellent customer service, faster response times, and valuable support for their customers. Lean can help to optimize all service delivery processes by targeting wastes and either removing them completely or move to a more effective state as part of a journey of continuous improvement.

An IT company, for example, is very different from a manufacturing company; however it still has many wasteful processes that could be removed or reduced. Lean tools and techniques can improve the customer experience by reducing unnecessary activities such as the number of call transfers and unnecessary IT processes while also providing solutions to cut down on errors, maximize employee empowerment, and become more cost-effective.

Financial firms are a prime example of a service sector that cannot afford to be wasteful, due to strong competition, the impact of the recent financial crisis, and vulnerability to economic downturns. Yet, it is claimed that at least 40 percent of costs in the financial sector are spent on wasteful activities that have no added value to the customer. Although they cannot control the fluctuating economy, financial companies can however invest in refining and redefining their own operations to ensure more effective and customer-focused operation.

Lean thinking can provide businesses such as banks, insurance, and investment companies with more productive and cost-effective solutions, therefore reducing risk during an economic dip. Lean would also help to improve employee satisfaction, increase customer value, and ensure the supporting activities are focused on delivering value.

Marketing companies have so many different processes to their business that without effective coordination in place, mistakes can easily occur. Every task needs to include a thorough process of planning, writing, designing, and proofing to generate a high enough standard of quality for their clients. These ongoing processes are not only extremely time-consuming, but with different tasks being assigned to different departments, project efficiency could also be compromised.

Lean implementation can help marketing companies to streamline their processes by removing tasks that are unnecessary and implementing a much more efficient approach. In doing so, lean also provides a direct improvement on work quality and therefore provides added value for the customer. This allows lean marketing companies to have that added edge over their competitors.

16.10 Case Study: McDonald's Lean Kitchen Area

Lean is defined as a process optimization methodology that focuses on improving the effectiveness and efficiency of a business process by eliminating activities that do not add value to the customers of the organization.

Lean can help service organizations to achieve significant performance improvement. The improvement can be in many dimensions including quality, productivity, cost-efficiencies, and profitability and customer satisfaction.

Service organizations are struggling with customer demands for better quality service and managerial demands for cost reduction. McDonalds is undertaking regular approaches in order to improve the service levels. These workshops are aiming to improve Lean Services and thus to reduce cost. The Lean Services are conducted by lean experts with employees. Based on this concept of permanently Lean Services McDonalds could permanently improve the performance of its employees and operations.

Since the early days of lean, it has been well proven that organizations of any size generally operate with around 90 percent of process-oriented "waste" leaving a mere 10 percent of value-added activity delivering services to their customers.

Lean was developed and implemented by the Toyota Manufacturer between 1945 and 1970. Lean was introduced as an alternative approach to mass production techniques. Lean led to raise productivity and quality levels by allowing flexibility of "skilled" production with the volume efficiencies of "mass" manufacturing.

The McDonald brothers, in 1948, closed their restaurant San Bernardino, California, for 3 months, reopening it in December as a walk-up hamburger stand that sold hamburgers, potato chips, and orange juice, and created the "fast-food" concept. This is probably the first lean service implementation in food sector.

16.10.1 Self-Development of Lean Kitchen Area

The McDonald's company has specialists who design the kitchen area themselves, integrating their acquired knowledge into a lean assembly line-style layout that maximized efficiency and output.

16.10.2 Automated Orders from Customers

McDonald's produces food under highly automated and controlled conditions. What is important to understand about this remarkably successful organization is not only that it has created a highly sophisticated piece of technology but also that it has done this by applying a manufacturing style of thinking to a people-intensive service situation. If machinery is to be viewed as a piece of equipment with the capability of producing a predictably standardized, customer-satisfying output while minimizing the operating discretion of its attendant, that is what a McDonald's retail outlet is. It is a machine that produces, with the help of totally unskilled machine tenders, a highly polished service.

16.10.3 Warming Bins

In the "Made for You" production system, there are no more warming trays. Each sandwich is prepared when the order is received from the customer. Yes, McDonald's sandwiches are more lean. This "Made for You" production system targets under 90 seconds from order to delivery and that includes 11 seconds of waiting for the superfast toaster!

In now, the McDonald's invest in front desk automation. Customers place their order at touch screens and then receive a number with a "digital locator", which then notifies staff to where the customer is sitting. Once the order is ready to serve, a McDonald's employee delivers the food to the customer's table.

16.10.4 Lean Processes and Standardized Material

The company uses a and standardized and simplified menu and food preparation using assembly flow principles. This allows the company to produce hamburgers on demand and on customer orders. The order-on-demand system is a pull system, in which every requested item is produced individually for each customer. The limited menu helps the company to achieve economies of scale in the upstream business, too. As a result the process and procurement cost are very low (Fig. 16.2).

Fig. 16.2 McDonald's lean operations. (Source: Author's Source)

References

Helmold, M., & Samara, W. (2019). *Progress in performance management. Industry insights and case studies on principles, application tools, and practice*. Heidelberg: Springer.

Helmold, M., & Terry, B. (2016). *Global sourcing and supply management excellence in China. Procurement guide for supply experts*. Singapore: Springer.

Rudnika, J. (2018). Statistik der Dienstleistungsbranche. Statista. Retrieved 1.12.2019. https://de.statista.com/statistik/daten/studie/255682/umfrage/bruttowertschoepfung-nach-wirtschaftsbereichen/.

Lean Management in Healthcare Sector 17

The starting point for improvement is to recognize the need.

Masaaki Imai (1930-today)

17.1 Lean Thinking in Healthcare Sector

Lean starts from the refusal to accept waste as defined by several authors like Helmold and Samara, Ohno, or Liker. Credited to Taiichi Ohno the lean system was developed through the 1950s and 1960s to provide the best quality, lowest cost, and shortest lead time through the elimination of waste. The Japanese term for what American companies usually categorize as waste is muda and was defined by Fujio Cho of Toyota as "Anything other than the minimum amount of equipment, space and worker's time, which are absolutely essential to add value to the product". The presence of these types of waste in a system has a negative impact on lead-time, cost, and quality. In the early 1980s, companies in other sectors like the healthcare sector have understood that the introduction of lean principles will lead to several advantages. Waste in healthcare can be described, among other elements, in excessive transport of medicine or patients, waiting time for treatments or underutilization of equipment and machines in hospitals. Moreover, duplications and inefficiencies by nurses may also impact the creation of waste.

17.2 Waste in Healthcare Sector

17.2.1 Lean Management and Waste in Healthcare

Although the lean business improvement methodology was initially developed to improve the quality and productivity of automotive factories, it has been used with

M. Helmold, *Lean Management and Kaizen*, Management for Professionals,
https://doi.org/10.1007/978-3-030-46981-8_17

great success in industries and settings of all types, including software development, government, retail, and other service settings.

Healthcare organizations, in particular, have found that the approach can be used to reduce costs and improve quality and patient satisfaction at the same time (Millard 2017). One of the core principles of lean is the elimination of waste, which is defined as anything that doesn't add value to the customer. Practitioners target eight specific types of waste (there were originally seven – more on that later). They are as common in healthcare as they are in manufacturing. Lean management targets therefore the elimination like waiting times or overmedication as outlined in Fig. 17.1 (Gupta 2013).

17.2.2 Transport

The waste of transportation occurs when materials are moved around inefficiently. In healthcare it occurs when:

- Patients are moved from department to department or room to room
- Medication is moved from the pharmacy to where it is needed
- Supplies are moved from storage to the floor

Some of this transportation is considered "necessary" waste to be minimized, even if it can't be completely eliminated.

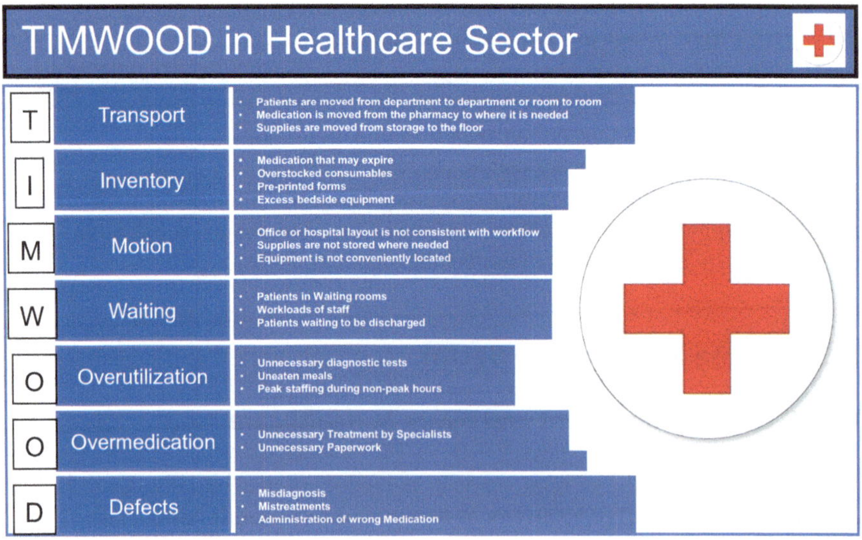

Fig. 17.1 TIMWOOD Concept in Healthcare-Sector. (Source: Author's Source)

17.2.3 Inventory

Manufacturers have largely moved to a just-in-time approach to inventory in order to reduce costs related to storage, movement, spoilage, and wastage. Healthcare organizations look to do the same as it relates to:

- Medication that may expire
- Overstocked consumables
- Pre-printed forms
- Excess bedside equipment

17.2.4 Motion

Motion refers to unnecessary movement of people within a facility or campus. This happens when:

- Office or hospital layout is not consistent with workflow
- Supplies are not stored where needed
- Equipment is not conveniently located

The first step in combating the wastes of lean is recognizing them within your organization. For most, examining each of these specific frequent contributors to waste leads to the discovery of multiple opportunities for improvement. We can also strive to eliminate wasted motion (including clicks) in software systems.

17.2.5 Waiting

In manufacturing, waiting occurs when parts can't flow or when team members can't perform their tasks due to problems, such as a lack of inventory or equipment failure. Waiting in healthcare is a problem for both patients and providers.

- Patients in waiting rooms (or exam rooms)
- Staff members with uneven workloads waiting for their next task
- Emergency department patients and physicians waiting for test results
- ED patients waiting to be admitted to the hospital
- Patients waiting to be discharged once medically ready

17.2.6 Overutilization

Overproduction in manufacturing results in excess "work in process" or unsold inventory of "finished goods". It is more difficult to spot in healthcare, but it occurs when providers do more than is needed by the customer at this moment. It includes:

- Unnecessary diagnostic tests
- Uneaten meals
- Ordering medications that the patient doesn't need
- Peak staffing during non-peak hours

17.2.7 Overmedication

Over-processing means doing more work, making it more complex or more expensive than is necessary. It takes the form of:

- Ordering complex diagnostic imagery (MRI) when a simpler method would suffice (X-ray)
- Unnecessary paperwork
- Surgical intervention in lieu of an equally effective medical alternative
- Follow-up appointments that don't improve patient outcomes
- Treatment by specialists that could be done by primary providers

17.2.8 Defects

While defects in manufacturing are expensive and troublesome, in healthcare they can be deadly. They may include:

- Misdiagnosis
- Administration of incorrect medications
- Hospital acquired conditions
- Incorrect IDC codes

The waste includes the time spent creating a defect, reworking these defects, and inspecting these defects. Even though we consider inspection to be waste, we can't eliminate inspection altogether until we have a perfect defect-free process. Even Toyota still has final inspection in the year 2016, but they consider it to be waste that they'd hope to eliminate some day.

17.3 Case Study: Vivantes' Transformation and Saving Plan

Vivantes, the largest municipal hospital group in Germany, is now initiating a restructuring phase in Berlin after the refurbishment in order to maintain its profitability. The Vivantes – Network for Health GmbH – is a hospital operator in Berlin. The sole shareholder is the state of Berlin. The company was founded on January 1, 2001. According to Vivantes, Vivantes is Germany's largest municipal hospital group. In 11 operating theatres from 6 different specialist disciplines, we work inter-professionally and interdisciplinary close and trusting together to ensure the safety and satisfaction of our patients at the highest level (Vivantes 2008). The team of the surgical coordination steers the surgical program and the daily routine in constant co-operation with all occupational groups involved in the surgical procedure. In doing so, we continuously monitor the processes for process optimization and keep statistics on planned stability and emergency emergencies. Vivantes CEO Joachim Bovelet showed in a shareholder meeting the Group's development concept, we will write in the coming years, no positive annual result, if we do not change. "He outlined the difficult conditions for hospitals in general and the particular historical structure of Vivantes with nine formerly urban clinics of the capital. The Supervisory Board and the Management Board of Vivantes use this concept as a strategy for the entire Group. They expect an efficiency improvement of 50 million euros if all measures are implemented. By 2015, the total operating area is to be reduced by around 20 percent to 550,000 square meters. Currently, at 130 square meters per patient, they are twice as high as in an optimized new building.

At the same time, it is planned that individual clinics will be merged into larger units, because the average size of Vivantes' clinics is well below the optimal size of 60 beds. Another goal is to reduce the comparatively high proportion of personnel costs by around 70 percent through process optimization. It also checks which medical activities can be transferred to nursing staff and which nursing work can be transferred to medical assistants. The expansion of outpatient services is also planned. A medical care centre (MVZ) or specialist centre is to be created at each location. Bovelet puts less emphasis on the opening of clinics in accordance with Article 116b SGB V: "The now wide opening of the clinics will be relativized, and it cannot compete with the residents but only with them", said the Vivantes boss. That also applies to the MVZ. The Group also wants to expand its range of comfort and optional services and the promising field of geriatric medicine. However, a detailed medical concept for the restructuring still has to be worked out. For the individual locations, the concept has different consequences. For example, the large Vivantes clinics are to be expanded, while smaller ones rather than simple "neighbourhood care providers" continue to be developed, and the Klinikum Prenzlauer Berg is completely converted into an outpatient centre. Uncertain is the future of the two Vivantes clinics in southwestern Berlin. For them and the campus Benjamin Franklin of the Charité, a common development concept of Charité and Vivantes is to be presented soon.

References

Gupta, D. (2013). Queueing models for healthcare operations. In B. T. Denton (Ed.), *Handbook of healthcare operations management. Methods and applications*. Heidelberg: Springer.

Millard, M. (2016). *The 7 wastes of lean in healthcare*. Retrieved 22 Nov 2019. https://blog.kainexus.com/improvement-disciplines/lean/7-wastes-of-lean-in-healthcare.

Vivantes. (2008). *Unternehmen. Vivantes strukturiert um für höhere Effizienz*. Ärztezeitung. Retrieved 22 Nov 2019. https://www.aerztezeitung.de/Wirtschaft/Vivantes-strukturiert-um-fuer-hoehere-Effizienz-354420.html.

Lean Management in the Education Sector 18

I never teach my students, I only attempt to provide the conditions in which they can learn.

Albert Einstein (1879–1955)

18.1 Importance of Lean Management in Education

18.1.1 Opportunities of Lean Activities in Education

Leaders who first brought up the idea of applying lean to the educational sector were confronted with some unexpected pushbacks. Many academics and practitioners consider lean as a concept within production and operations, where it was first developed by Toyota in Japan. It was assumed that the goal of lean management was to create something of an assembly line in universities, colleges, or schools. As both groups, teachers and scholars, dislike the idea of education as a kind of assembly line and factory for mass production, the resistance was quite high.

Fortunately, lean management is not assembly line or production thinking. Lean management is focused on the elimination of waste and the continuous improvement and the perfection of activities and processes. That means that all primary and secondary activities from enrolment, induction, teaching, or graduation have to be analysed in terms of waste and value-added activities. Based on this evaluation, processes can be revised and streamlined in order to be lean. The same applies to the organization and reporting structures in universities, colleges, or schools (Helmold and Samara 2019).

As educational institutes do not produce tangible products (like a factory), it is important to combine any service with tangible evidence. Examples are that university should have graduation ceremonies with all passed students to be awarded, best thesis award, and the mentioning of special performance during the course or

M. Helmold, *Lean Management and Kaizen*, Management for Professionals,
https://doi.org/10.1007/978-3-030-46981-8_18

semester. Certainly, universities certainly produce measurable results in terms of student achievement that can be monitored and improved over time. Lean concepts can certainly be applied to teaching practices within schools, but it is important also to think about all of the processes that surround what happens in the classroom. Universities have functions like:

- Marketing
- International affairs
- Accounting
- Emergency preparedness
- Human resources
- Facility maintenance
- Budgeting
- Food service
- Technology
- Professional development
- Certification
- Fundraising
- Testing
- Parent/community relations
- Communications
- Office administration
- Transportation
- Reporting

18.1.2 Lean Management Beyond Administration

Universities and teaching institutions that want to apply lean management to their operations should consider how they can affect a larger portion of their teaching staff and the teaching process as a whole, instead of focusing on the administrative layer of the school/university. Basically, are the administrators leading the teachers using lean principles and concepts (coaching and mentoring), or are they using traditional management methods (telling them what to do)? This is still a major problem in some places trying to apply lean. The important thing is that lean continues to see adoption in as many institutions as possible (both in the administration and in the classroom), so that more minds can work on evolving its ideas and pushing the whole concept forward.

Lecturers and teachers should be open in expressing their concerns about this as well. It's not rare that the teaching staff of the school would just accept the new situation without voicing any concerns about it, and this can lead to a cascading effect, where everyone continues to be disappointed by the way things are evolving. Using proper change management techniques is essential to making improvements in education. In fact, obtaining feedback from teachers, and using that to improve the way the school operates, is an excellent place for an improvement program to get started.

Considering that communication is one of the main points of impact addressed by lean, an institution that applies these ideas properly should see continuous improvement instead of continuing to run into the same problems. Lean can be a major boost to the productivity of any education organization that applies it properly, regardless of the size of the school or number of students. The important thing is that the main concepts behind lean are applied to all levels of the education, from students to teachers to administration, parent organizations, and support staff (janitorial, cafeteria, maintenance, etc.). The goal should be to allow all employees to provide their input on ways to make the education better for the students.

18.1.3 Lean Management in Education

Lean practitioners in schools include staff members in every department and at every level to document current practices, define opportunities for improvement, and implement positive change to each process that contributes to the delivery of education service. Usually, an incremental approach to change is employed to streamline tasks, reduce resource needs, and control costs.

Lean is not a new burden or extra work for employees. It is a methodology that ultimately empowers workers to contribute ideas on how to make their work more effective and efficient. One of the central tenants of the approach is respect for people. The idea is to practice bottom-up management, giving the frontline employees, who are closest to every-day challenges, the support they need to solve problems quickly. The process of improvement in a lean education environment is simple, yet powerful. Employees identify and report opportunities for improvement, preferably using lean software. Then an improvement cycle commonly referred to as PDSA (Plan, Do, Study, Adjust). The team agrees on a theory of what to do to achieve a specific improvement (Plan), the new idea is implemented (Do), the results are analysed (Study), adjustments are made if necessary, and a new standard is deployed for the process (Adjust). Once complete, a new cycle of improvement can begin, creating a continuous flow of small gains. There is no magic wand that can be used to make a school or district suddenly a lean machine. There are a few things that need to be in place in order to get the most impactful results.

Leadership: Although lean is a bottom-up concept, strong leadership is essential for success. Leaders set the tone and provide support and resources. The best results with lean come from deep commitment, which starts at the top.

Culture: Lean is a team sport that should impact the way every employee, from teachers to maintenance engineers, approaches problems. Employees should be rewarded and recognized for engagement and everyone should see improvement as part of their job responsibilities.

Training: The lean approach has been around for a long time and has been broadly used. There are tons of valuable lessons that have already been learned. With the right training, lean leaders in education can build on what's happened in manufacturing, healthcare, and technology companies rather than reinvent the wheel.

Technology: These days, if something is important, there's a software application to support it. That's true in lean as well. The right solution helps increase the momentum of change, improve the impact, and prove the value of the work.

The benefits of lean in education can be profound. It isn't the only solution to the challenges faced by educators today, but we predict it will significantly contribute to improving educational outcomes and job satisfaction.

18.2 Case Study: Mission and Sustainability in IUBH University

With a world population of 7 billion people and limited natural resources, we, as individuals and societies, need to learn to live together sustainably. We need to take action responsibly based on the understanding that what we do today can have implications on the lives of people and the planet in the future. Education for Sustainable Development (ESD) empowers people to change the way they think and work towards a sustainable future. UNESCO aims to improve access to quality education on sustainable development at all levels and in all social contexts, to transform society by reorienting education and help people develop knowledge, skills, values, and behaviours needed for sustainable development. It is about including sustainable development issues, such as climate change and biodiversity into teaching and learning. Individuals are encouraged to be responsible actors who resolve challenges, respect cultural diversity, and contribute to creating a more sustainable world. The German Federal Ministry of Education and Research (BMBF) and the German Commission of UNESCO (DUK) awarded the "Bad Honnef studies Sustainability" network (to which IUBH also belongs) for its excellent contribution as part of the UNESCO World Action Program "Education for Sustainable Development" in 2019. With limited natural resources, we at IUBH believe in the importance of learning to live sustainably. From the courses offered on campus to our publications, we believe we can have a ripple effect on industries and the world for the better. The network is already firmly established in Bad Honnef and the region and is committed to raising the awareness of sustainability, climate, and environmental protection among adults, young people, and children alike. In addition to the International University of Applied Sciences Bad Honnef (IUBH), the city of Bad Honnef, the sewage works of the city of Bad Honnef and the Bad Honnef AG belong to the network. The IUBH has the following mission statement (see Fig. 18.1): "In service to the international management potentials. The profile requirements of internationally employed managers have changed. We recognised this as the first private, state-recognised university operating exclusively in the service sector. With our attractive Bachelor and Master's degree courses we want to set new standards for the new generation of management. Our programmes are characterised by the effective transfer of subject-specific knowledge and soft skills in order to prepare our

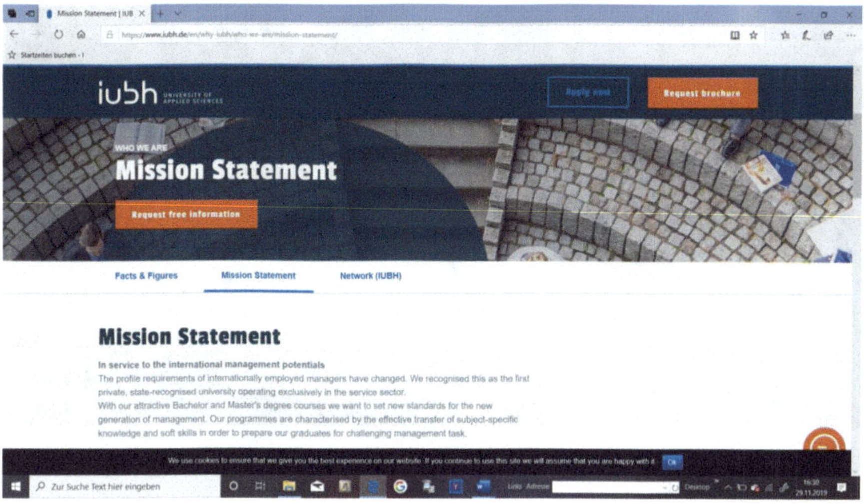

Fig. 18.1 Mission Statement of the IUBH International University. (Source: www.iubh.de)

graduates for challenging management task". The following four key success factors are important for the implementation of the IUBH strategy:

Internationality: The IUBH is geared to the demands of the global market. Studying at the IUBH makes careers in a global environment possible. We live out this credo in that English is the teaching language and the language used on our campus. We also impart internationality with many other distinguishing features: our experts and faculty from around the world teach both technical know-how and soft skills. We maintain multiple collaborations with partner universities in Europe, America, Australia, and Asia. At the IUBH languages in international demand are taught at advanced levels by native speakers, and additional intercultural communication competence is developed. There are currently students from over 85 countries on our campuses. For our students, our international commitment pays off in many ways. Approx. 75 percent of our graduates work successfully in an international environment.

Practical Relevance: The close integration of theory and practice ensures excellent career prospects. At the IUBH practical orientation is experienced first-hand. The curriculum has multiple facets which reflect this, for example, the inclusion of internship semesters, discussions, and lectures with experts from industry and excursions to companies. The integration of theory and practice is a daily reality for every student. In the context of its lectures the IUBH offers project work and case studies. Many of the benefits of studying at the IUBH are possible due to the close cooperation that the IUBH and its faculty maintain with industry. Our faculty has contact to all DAX 30 companies and is recognized in the international market and well connected in a network with over 1000 business partners.

Fig. 18.2 Lean Training in Class in IUBH International University. (Source: Author's Source)

Reputation and Quality: Numerous certificates and awards confirm the excellent IUBH reputation.

On a regular basis the IUBH achieves top scores in evaluations. Reputable accreditations, partnerships, and memberships indicate the high quality of the university and its programmes.

In 2009, as part of its institutional accreditation, the IUBH received the highest seal of quality from the German Council of Science and Humanities (Wissenschaftsrat): unconditional accreditation for 10 years. The IUBH is accredited by the Foundation of International Business Administration Accreditation (FIBAA) and received for five of its study programmes five golden FIBAA premium seals so far. Therefore, the IUBH is one of the leading universities in Germany to be awarded five or more premium seals. In 2012 the IUBH also received the seal of quality from the Hanseatic Certification Agency which certified IUBH study programmes as a way to obtain vocational education and training.

Figure 18.2 shows pictures of the Performance Management class of the master course, in which students learn about lean management principles by establishing a model factory. In three or four rounds, the students assemble plugs and improve step-by-step by applying 5S, poka-yoke or JIT principles.

Other examples of lean tools in education can be seen in Fig. 18.3. The figure shows best practices of the IUBH in terms of visualization and 5S. It is visible that tools like markers, remote control for the beamers in class rooms, magnets, and wipers are pre-sorted for lecturers. As a result, lecturers and teachers can quickly take advantage and concentrate on teaching instead of preparation. The class kits are available at the entrance and can be taken on the way to the classroom. Another best practice is the 5S cleaning and inspection before the classes start. Rooms must be cleaned, flip charts must be available, and in winter rooms are pre-heated.

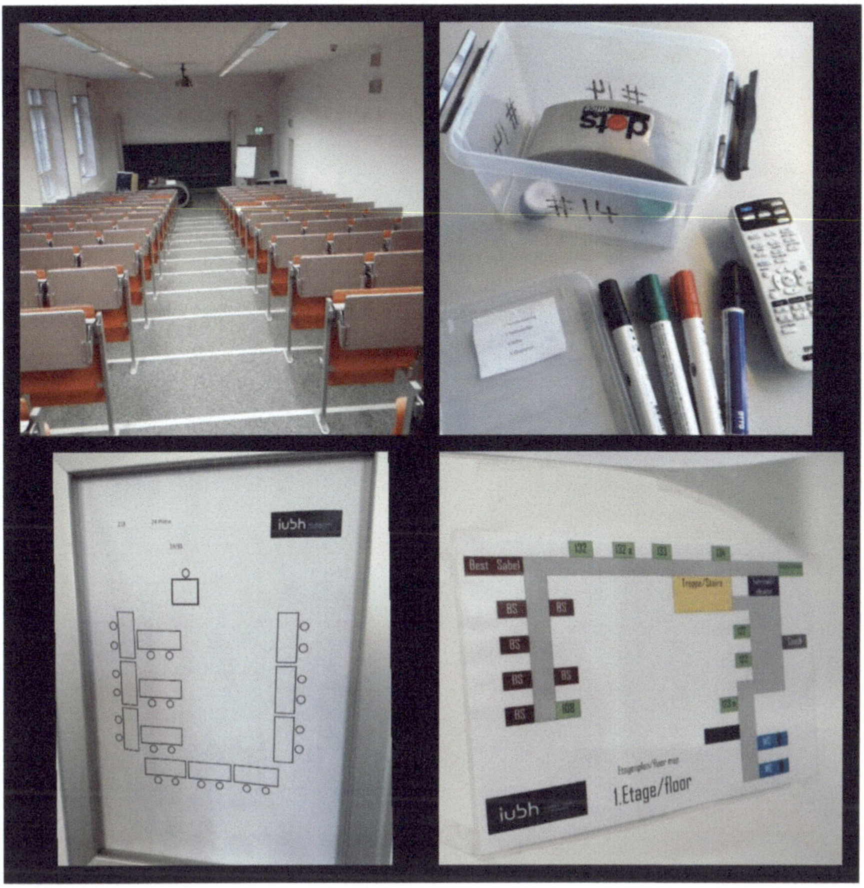

Fig. 18.3 Lean management examples in IUBH International University. (Source: Author's Source)

These tasks are done by administrative staff, so that the lecturers can concentrate on teaching. The last best practice examples show visualization of the layout in the class and directions to the class rooms.

Reference

Helmold, M., & Samara, W. (2019). *Progress in performance management. Industry insights and case studies on principles, application tools, and practice*. Heidelberg: Springer.

19 Lean Audits and Quality Management Systems (QMS)

There are two kinds of people, those who do the work and those who take the credit. Try to be in the first group; there is less competition there.

Indira Gandhi (1917–1984)

19.1 Lean Audits

19.1.1 Audit Types

Audits can be described as a systematic and structured performance evaluation and assessment of a system, process, or product or any other area by internal or external auditors. The aim of an audit is to evaluate and approve or disapprove the assessed area by standardized criteria and questions, to define areas for actions, and to ensure the sustainable implementation of the actions and improvement areas. Assessment criteria in audits are based on customer and stakeholder expectations. Audits can be clustered in systems, process, product, control, and special audits as shown in Table 19.1. Lean audits are conducted to determine if the business is properly implementing and lean management methodologies are implemented into the company and value chain (Helmold and Terry 2016). This is achieved by a detailed 360 degrees analysis how lean processes with a goal towards recognizing opportunities to improve processes and to eliminate waste.

19.1.2 Quality Management Systems (QMS)

A quality management system (QMS) describes in enterprises and organizations the management function and all organizational activities, which serve the

M. Helmold, *Lean Management and Kaizen*, Management for Professionals,
https://doi.org/10.1007/978-3-030-46981-8_19

Table 19.1 Audit types

Audit type	Description
Systems audit	Evaluation of the quality management system of organizations by external certification agencies (TÜV, DEKRA) Examples: DIN EN ISO 9001:2015, TS 16949, International Railway Industry Standard (IRIS) or IATF 16949
Process audit	Evaluation of a (manufacturing or service) process to qualify or disqualify a process-oriented example of a product or service by assessing a reference process from supply side, incoming material to the despatch (also from other customers) Examples: VDA 6.3, SEAP (Railway)
Product audit	Planning and execution of the assessment of a finished product to be delivered to the customer. The audit consists of checking the specification, drawings, capacity, and other important aspects and normally involves the trial run of the entire manufacturing process (e.g. 300 parts, run at rate) Examples: VDA 6.5, Part Production Approval Process (PPAP), Production Approval Process (PAP)
Control audit	Control audits aim to control the progress of previously conducted audits
Other audits	Any other audits in areas like safety, health, environment, tax, and financials Examples: 5S audits, tax audits, environmental audits (ISO 14001), IT audits (ISO 27001), financial audits or health, safety and environment (HSE) audits

Table 19.2 QMS

QMS norm	Industry
ISO 9001:2015	General quality management system
VDA 6.1	Automotive industry
IATF 16949	Automotive industry
IRIS	Railway industry
EN 9100	Aerospace industry
ISO 13485	Medical industry
TL 9000	Telecommunications industry

Source: Author's own table

improvement of the process quality, the work quality, and thus the product and service quality. QMS are using lean features for process improvements. Table 19.2 outlines the most common standards of QMS in certain industries.

19.2 Case Study: 5S Audits in Berliner Kindl Schultheiss Brewery

With 5S audits, the Berliner Kindl Schultheiss Brewery (Radeberger Group) makes sure that all processes (purchasing, operations, logistics, production control, and planning) are evaluated along the seven most important levers for their optimization. On the basis of these results, further measures can be derived on the way to a lean and smart production. With the audit, the management receives an objective assessment of lean. It includes 2 days of on-site operation and is conducted in the form of a walk-through with short interviews with the people in charge. At the end of the second day the results will be presented. Several lean performance indicators are measured through this approach, which also give an idea of the lean maturity. The evaluation of the respective dimensions is based on a SWOT analysis (Helmold and Samara 2019). The lean audit provides a solid basis for planning further project steps. Thus, the identified potentials can be used for a workshop to develop appropriate target states and measures. Finally, in order to achieve this, there is an extensive set of methods in the context of the Schneider co-developed lean-factory design concept. This interdisciplinary optimization concept, developed at Landshut University of Applied Sciences, is based on many years of research and numerous best practice projects. The audit can be repeated annually to measure project progress and to set and prioritize the following steps.

The Berliner Kindl Schultheiss Brewery conducts the 5S audits on a monthly basis as shown in Fig. 19.1. It can be seen that the five categories (sort, set in order, shine, standardize, sustain) are analysed. The audit is linked to a dynamic action plan and progress control.

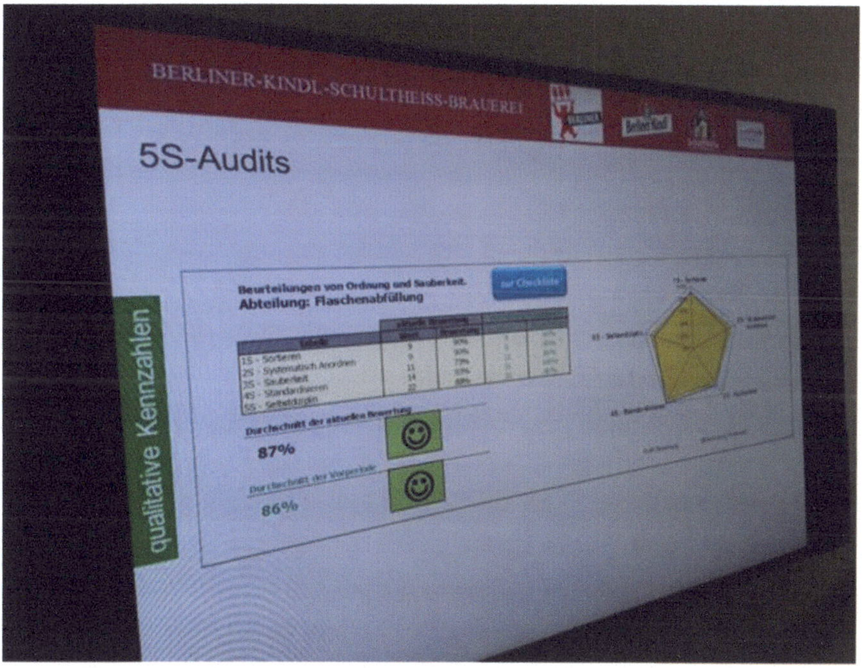

Fig. 19.1 5S audit in Berliner Kindl Schultheiss Brewery. (Source: Author's Source)

References

Helmold, M., & Samara, W. (2019). Progress in performance management. Industry insights and case studies on principles, application tools, and practice. Heidelberg: Springer.

Helmold, M., & Terry, B. (2016). *Global sourcing and supply management excellence in China. Procurement guide for supply experts*. Singapore: Springer.

Outlook of Lean Management 20

Simplicity is the ultimate Sophistication.

Leonardo da Vinci (1452–1519)

20.1 Lean Management and Industry 4.0

For several decades, manufacturers have used lean principles and tools to reduce operational complexity and improve productivity. The lean approach provides the foundation for operational excellence by standardizing processes, instilling a culture of continuous improvement, and empowering workers on the shop floor. However, given the increasing complexity of operations, many companies have found that lean management by itself is not sufficient to address their operational challenges. Recently, a set of advanced digital technologies known as Industry 4.0 has emerged to offer new approaches for dealing with complexity and improving productivity. By deploying the right combination of technologies, manufacturers can boost speed, efficiency, and coordination and even facilitate self-managing factory operations. Manufacturers seeking to optimize their operations need to understand the interplay between traditional lean management and Industry 4.0. Supporting hundreds of operational excellence programs in recent years, we have seen companies generate valuable synergies by implementing lean management and Industry 4.0 holistically, rather than independently or sequentially. Indeed, in most cases, the integrated application of lean management and Industry 4.0, which we call Lean Industry 4.0, is the most effective way to reach the next level of operational excellence. Innovative technologies promote the transparency, networking, and automation of business processes in the context of Industry 4.0 and offer a great deal of potential for companies in the manufacturing industry. This raises the question of how these new technologies can be brought together with the often already established lean management principles for process optimization and complexity

M. Helmold, *Lean Management and Kaizen*, Management for Professionals,
https://doi.org/10.1007/978-3-030-46981-8_20

reduction. A recent study by the management consultancy Bearingpoint shows that the successful use of lean management 4.0 differs greatly depending on the industry (Bearingpoint 2019). Decision-makers from 50 companies in the manufacturing industry were asked about the progress within their environment. The focus was on the four functional areas: production, logistics, purchasing, and sales. Digital progress makes a key contribution to the sustainable implementation of lean management, which in turn is a key success factor for the implementation of Industry 4.0. According to the study, more than two-thirds of the respondents (72 percent) confirm the potential of digitization to further and sustainably streamline business processes. Nevertheless, many companies are still in the beginning and learning stages of implementing digital technologies and lean management methods. The biggest obstacles are inflexible processes (26 percent) and hierarchical structures (21 percent). Further challenges are conservative corporate strategies and limited financial resources (12 percent each). To take full advantage of the benefits of digital transformation and make sure you do not miss it, it's not enough just to see the potential; companies need to be prepared to adapt structurally and processually to new circumstances – an important step to success They are sophisticated lean management and lean processes in all industrial functional areas, and the latter need to identify and implement the right digital technologies (Siebenmorgen 2016).

20.2 Lean Management 2030

Lean management tools of the future (Lean Management 2030) will help companies to make complex and global value streams transparent and manageable. Lean provides standardized tools and methods that help companies focus on customer value and enable each individual employee to actively engage and continuously improve (Bertagnolli 2018). But what if humans no longer have the opportunity to survey the complexity and thereby continuously bring in ideas for improvement? Big Data and additive manufacturing as exemplary drivers of digitization are also used in manufacturing companies and used in sectors like Healthcare or Service Industry. A continuous roll-out to other industries of technologies will be visible within the next 10 years. Manufacturers that have successfully already deployed Lean Industry 4.0 can further reduce conversion costs by as much as 40 percent in 5–10 years to be fit for Lean Management 2030, considerably better than the reductions captured by best-in-class independent deployment of lean or Industry 4.0. The higher cost reductions are, in many cases, achieved with technologies that improve plant processes and structures by, for example, optimizing layouts. (See Fig. 20.1, BCG Focus, December 2016.) However, fewer than 5 percent of the manufacturing companies that we have observed have reached a high level of maturity in Lean Industry 4.0. To capture the greatest benefits, a manufacturer must tailor the application of Lean Industry 4.0 to address its specific challenges along the supply chain and at the plant level. A recent global survey by the Boston Consulting Group found that leading industrial companies recognize the importance of both lean management and digitalization in their long-term planning. In a survey of more than 750 production

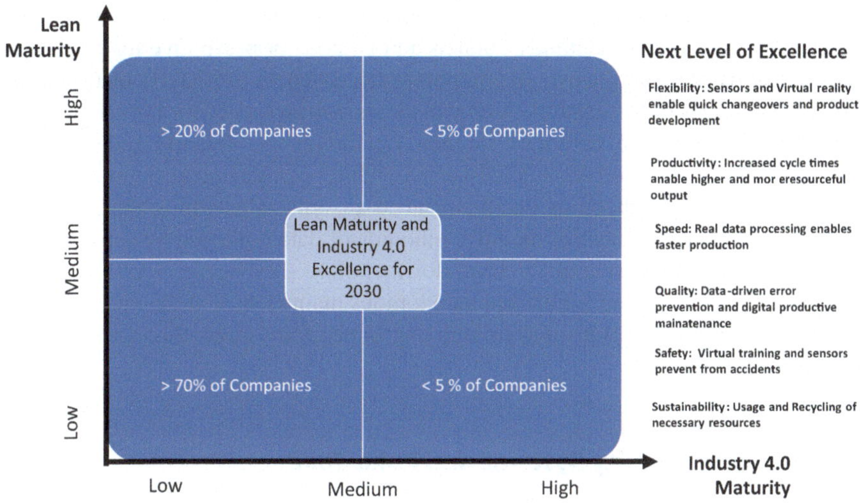

Fig. 20.1 Lean Factory 2030. (Source: Own Source, adjusted from BCG)

managers, 97 percent of automotive respondents said that lean management would be highly relevant in 2030, compared with 70 percent who said that it is important today. Among these respondents, 70 percent said that plant digitalization would be highly relevant in 2030, compared with 13 percent who said that it is important today (Küpper et al. 2017).

20.2.1 Flexible Sensors and Software

Manufacturers want flexible operations that allow them to use one production line to make multiple products. However, the benefits of flexibility are hard to capture because time-consuming changeovers are required to prepare machinery to manufacture different products. By implementing lean tools, such as single-minute exchange of dies, manufacturers can remove non-value-adding activities from the changeover, thus significantly accelerating the process. Companies that implemented lean methods and industry 4.0 will be able to benefit from these technologies (Küpper et al. 2017). New sensors and software make it possible for machines to automatically identify products and load the appropriate program and tools without manual intervention. Because the changeover is automated, operators can focus on performing value-adding activities.

20.2.2 Predictive Algorithms and Virtual Maintenance

Lean management in 2030 will include algorithms and virtual tools. In many manufacturing industries, equipment breakdowns and failures lead to high inventory levels, significant working capital cost, and low efficiency (Küpper et al. 2017). Companies can use lean methods, such as autonomous or preventive maintenance, to significantly increase the overall equipment effectiveness (OEE). By using autonomous maintenance, for example, companies assign responsibility for specific do-it-yourself maintenance activities to their operators, significantly reducing the downtime required to correct minor issues. Leading manufacturers are making the most of these lean methods by using advanced analytics algorithms and machine-learning techniques to analyse the huge amounts of data collected by sensors. The output identifies the potential for breakdowns before they occur. Such predictive insights prepare operators to perform autonomous maintenance at the optimal time, thereby reducing disruptions and minimizing unnecessary downtime and replacement costs.

20.2.3 Digital Quality Systems and Poka-Yoke

Lean Management 2030 methodologies will use digital error prevention appliances. Production capacity is wasted if products do not meet specifications. Even worse, if a company ships poor-quality products to customers, they will incur higher costs and likely lose trust in that supplier. Many lean management tools, such as self-inspection, poka-yoke, and jidoka, have been developed to reduce the probability of mistakes and increase the rate and speed of error detection. For example, the analysis by Boston Consulting Group shows that self-inspections improve the process of providing feedback to engineers and operators, thereby accelerating error detection and reducing the number of defects by 50–70 percent. However, to achieve zero defects, manufacturers must support self-inspections by using a data-driven analytics approach to identify the root causes of errors. Industry 4.0 technologies and innovative lean methods allow such support by providing reliable context data and the ability to conduct detailed tracking. The analysis of errors is enhanced through, for example, camera-based visual inspection, correlation models, and real-time monitoring of process parameters (Küpper et al. 2017).

20.2.4 Digital Human Resources and Automated Training

Elements of health, safety, and environment (HSE) are among the most important production paradigms. To ensure operator safety, one lean approach uses signs to tell operators where they may walk. Another lean approach uses detailed tracking of incidents and near misses to identify areas for improvement. Companies can use low-cost wireless sensors to improve the effectiveness of such efforts. For example, they can fit operators with sensors that will alert them to the presence of dangerous gases or the possibility of a clash with nearby forklifts or trucks. Companies can further improve safety by using virtual reality to train workers. Offsite training in a virtual environment is more efficient and effective than training in an actual work environment, and the approach appeals to the younger generation of workers.

Seeking to reduce the high accident rate among new hires, a provider of service rigs developed immersive-training sessions in which workers practice often-dangerous tasks in a virtual simulation of the work site (Küpper et al. 2017).

20.2.5 Digital Resource Planning and Sustainability

Future ERP systems will be integrated into the entire value chain from raw material makers to the final the end customers. Digitalization will enable a transparent and sustainable supply chain including departments like procurement, operations, marketing, planning, logistics, finance, human resources, and distribution (Helmold and Terry 2016).

20.3 Lean Management 2050

When it comes to the outlook for the future 30 years, one can say that lean management tools and processes will become more digitalized, virtual, and autonomous. After digitization as a megatrend has long been in the foreground, artificial intelligence (AI) is increasingly becoming the focus of technically induced social change. AI or KI (German: Künstliche Intelligenz) stands for a group of technologies and applications that implement intelligent and IT-based solutions based on digital infrastructures and often using mass or big data. At present, the focus is on user behaviour when shopping, in social media or in media consumption. Examples from everyday life are image and speech recognition, navigation and driver assistance systems, customized advertising, dating services, or translation programs, the results of which have become virtually error-free. Automated emergency detection, control of energy consumption, or remote control of household appliances is summarized under the term Smart Home. However, the applications of AI will have a significant impact on lean management and the digital synchronization of supply network systems. The use of artificial intelligence also extends into the artistic sphere and space. It is reported by machines that make images in the style of famous artists (Siebenmorgen 2016) or recognize composers. Where mass data is available on the Internet, which can be statistically analysed, patterned, computed, and used predictively by high-performance computers, the use of artificial intelligence is more likely than in areas where mass data is not available. Although the term AI was invented by John McCarthy at the Dartmouth Conference back in 1956 (Helmold and Samara 2019), it is only now, with the ever-increasing amount of available data and the development of computers, that it is unimaginable to reach unimaginable masses perform. There is a distinction between "weak AI" and "strong AI". Weak AI refers to technologies with strong application relevance and the goal of developing a very concrete solution in clearly defined, given problem contexts. All of today's AI systems fall into the category of this weak AI. The strong AI, in contrast, has a much wider and more ambitious goal: it attempts to mimic or even surpass the full intellectual ability of humans, regardless of a concrete problem context. It can be seen that AI and related technologies, on the one hand, are subject to high expectations, on the other hand, but also to defensive responses. The idea that machines can behave like humans and that all expressions of life as well as machines are connected to each other via the Internet leads to a new boom in dystopian expectations of the future. The discomfort of losing the idea of the uniqueness of human consciousness and control over the machines is supported by impresarios such as Stephen Hawking and Elon Musk, who see tremendous momentum in AI, capitalist monopolists dominating the market, and warnings speak out against abuse. In addition to the still unclear developments in society as a whole, sector-specific solutions are formulated and tested in concrete terms, e.g. in the working world (Smart Factory, Smart Office, Ambient Environment), in leisure time (chess computer, gaming, navigation), and in the health sector (smart devices for rehabilitation, diagnoses). Operations and lean processes will be designed in smaller environments and with devices, and this will be done our in everyday life. This raises the question of how and by what means new employment opportunities can be created. Major shifts are indicated in the industrial sector (Industry 4.0), in trade, but also in the media, jurisdiction, agriculture, or insurance (Siebenmorgen 2016). New professions are expected in the service, IT, and media sectors. Changes in favour of both low and high skilled occupations and elimination of intermediate skills are likely. As a necessary consequence of the expected job loss, a far-reaching restructuring of the social system in the direction of the unconditional basic income and a robot tax is discussed. Terms such as Smart Home, Smart Cities, Smart Region, and Smart Health summarize developments aimed at further developing technical and social infrastructures. Smart City comprises a city development in which the "large technical systems" are to be optimized, integrated, and monitored on the basis of digital networking. The processes of the municipalities are to be accelerated, made more transparent, and more inclusive by digital techniques, whereby participatory processes are modified. At the supra-local level, it is expected that the digital infrastructure will enable companies and workers to be kept or won. Cooperations and voting could be made easier, including mobility offers and mobility platforms.

Smart and lean Factory of the future will be able to produce the required amount of product while spending fewer resources than at present. One of the important aspects of the new industrial revolution is the ability to work with and to react on real-time demands in a systematic end-to-end supply chain process, which will direct the production of a significant reduction in the time form of instant just-in-time pull production. Data and virtual simulations will affect the optimization of ordering, planning, and production times significantly (Helmold and Samara 2019). In the lean management concept 2050, it is forecasted that flexible manufacturing facilities will occupy an integral part of the whole value chain and will be equipped with cyber-physical systems, which is a single whole of the Internet and the real physical objects. Such integration has significant advantages: the interaction with the environment, adapting a rapidly changing environment, rapid reconfiguration, and self-optimizing will lead to shorter lead times and the reduction of waste by a more resourceful process. Using a variety of sensors and built-in mechanisms has a significant impact on the structure optimization of the company, as well as it can lead to a substantial conservation of resources of the enterprise. This approach can further convert the production system into an environmentally safe, efficient advanced manufacturing.

20.4 Case Study: Lean Supply in Airbus Through AirSupply

Airbus SE, formerly Airbus Group SE, is a company based in the Netherlands that is active in the aerospace and defence industry. The company operates through three segments: Airbus Commercial Aircraft, Airbus Helicopters, and Airbus Defence and Space. The Airbus Commercial Aircraft segment focuses on the development, manufacturing, marketing, and sale of commercial jet aircraft and aircraft components, as well as on aircraft conversion and related services. The Airbus Helicopters segment specializes in the development, manufacturing, marketing, and sale of civil and military helicopters, as well as on the provision of helicopter related services. The Airbus Defence and Space segment produces military combat aircraft and training aircraft, provides defence electronics and global security market solutions, and manufacturers and markets missiles. For the commercial side, more than 75 percent of the value creation is done by suppliers. The suppliers are supplying components and systems, which are assembled to sub-systems by Airbus operational sites. These subassemblies are produced in four different countries and then shipped downstream to the final assembly as shown in Fig. 20.1. The subassemblies are delivered from different national sites to the final assembly lines. Airbus uses the AirSupply system, which integrates ERP systems on the downstream side. AirSupply is a single supply chain solution for direct deliveries to Airbus by its suppliers in the downstream supply chain (Siebenmorgen 2016). The integration of ERP systems makes the supply or value chain very transparent, so that actions for improvements can be allocated quickly to shortcomings. Additionally, the model enables to synchronize companies' manufacturing and logistics systems digitally and physically through the application of lean management tools (Helmold and Samara 2019). The portal is shared by the main European aerospace companies within the BoostAeroSpace hub. The AirSupply collaborative hub helps manufacturers and suppliers to gain visibility, as well as ensure control and integration for critical business processes. This common secured platform for European aerospace and defence industry players results from the BoostAeroSpace cooperation led by Airbus, Dassault Aviation, Safran, and Thales as shown in Fig. 20.2. It provides a single solution for the aerospace community connecting original equipment manufacturers (OEMs) and suppliers, standardized supply chain collaboration processes and shared formats for data exchange, and one platform for a single supply chain process collaboration via the Internet (Software-as-a-Service provided by SupplyOn, with worldwide service) (Fig. 20.3).

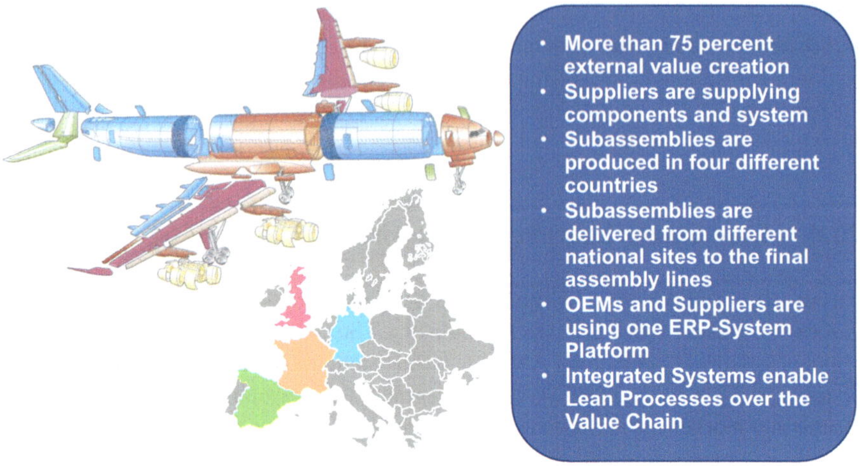

Fig. 20.2 AirSupply network. (Source: Author's own figure, adopted from SupplyOn)

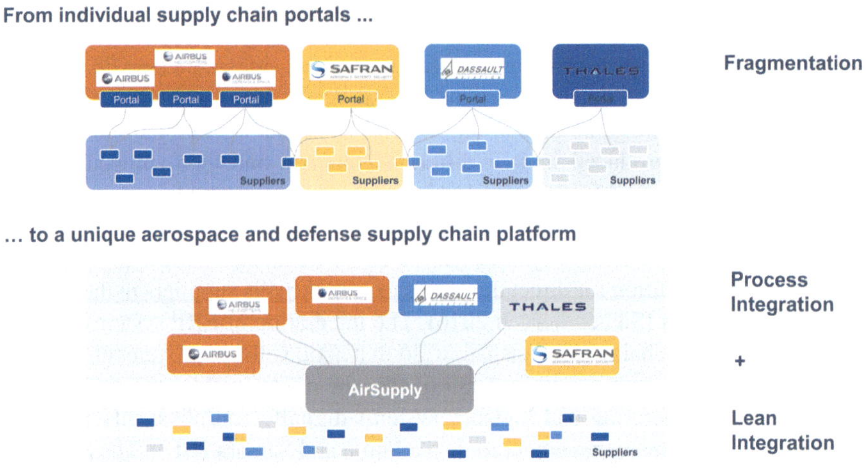

Fig. 20.3 AirSupply. (Source: Author's own figure, adopted from SupplyOn)

References

Bearingpoint. (2019). *Lean 4.0. Schlank durch Digitalisierung*. Retrieved 22 Nov 2019. https://www.it-production.com/allgemein/lean-4-0-schlank-durch-digitalisierung/.

Bertagnolli, F. (2018). *Lean management*. Wiesbaden: Springer.

Helmold, M., & Samara, W. (2019). *Progress in performance management. Industry insights and case studies on principles, application tools, and practice*. Heidelberg: Springer.

Helmold, M., & Terry, B. (2016). *Global sourcing and supply management excellence in China. Procurement guide for supply experts*. Singapore: Springer.

Küpper, D., et al. (2017). *When lean meets industry 4.0. The next level of operational excellence*. Boston Consulting Group. Retrieved 28 Nov 2019. https://www.bcg.com/publications/2017/lean-meets-industry-4.0.aspx.

Siebenmorgen, F. (2016). *Industrie 4.0. Das Potenzial schon heute nutzen*. Retrieved 28 Nov 2019. https://www.supplyon.com/wp-content/uploads/import/DE_SCM%20Magazin_Industrie%20 4.0.pdf.

Glossary of Lean Management Terms

Standards should not be forced down from above but rather set by the production workers themselves.

Taiichi Ohno (1912–1990)

A

Andon	アンドン Audio-visual tool in operations to stop the production
Ato Hoju	Replenishment system
Atokotei Hikitori	あとこうてい引き取り Pull system

B

Bacho	場所 Place, location
Baka	馬鹿 Stupid
Baka-Yoke	馬鹿 System to avoid any human and stupid mistake

C

Chaku Chaku Line	ちゃくちゃく Chaku Chaku is a way to operate a semi-automated manufacturing line. One (or more) worker walks around the line, adds parts to the processes, and then starts the process. While the process works on the part automatically, the worker adds the next part to the next process and so on.
Chiiku	(知育) Intellectual knowledge and develop logical thinking for fundamental survival skills
CSR	Corporate social responsibility Business model that helps a company be socially accountable

M. Helmold, *Lean Management and Kaizen*, Management for Professionals,
https://doi.org/10.1007/978-3-030-46981-8

D

Design for Manufacturing	Product development in line with the objectives to produce the part in an efficient and lean manner
Dou	道, マツダ道 Path, best way, road. Mazda way or mazda path

E

Engineering	Functional Department for Product Development
ERP	Enterprise Resource Planning

F

Flow Principle	Material is flowing between the operations

G

Gemba	現場 The real place, production shopfloor
Gembutsu	現場 Working on the right products
Genchi	現地 Working with the right facts

H

Heijunka	平準化 Levelling production

I

Ichiban	一番,いちばん The best, the most successful

J

Jidoka	自動化 *Jidoka* is one of the most important lean methods for ensuring built-in quality. The commonly used English word for jidoka is *auto***no***mation*, based on *autonomous* and *automation*. Others call it *intelligent automation*, and again others describe it as *automation with a human touch* (remember the additional character 人 for human)

K

Kaizen	改善 Change for the good Kaizen is a compound of two Japanese words that together translate as good change or improvement

Kanban	看板 Visual Planning System
KPI	Key performance indicators Quantified and numeric objectives
Learning, Studying	勉強 Continuous learning and studying

M

Mottainai	もったいない or 勿体無い A term of Japanese origin that has been used by environmentalists. The term in Japanese conveys a sense of regret over waste
Muda	無駄 Waste
Muri	無理 Unreasonableness; impossible; beyond one's power; too difficult; by force; perforce; forcibly; compulsorily; excessiveness; immoderation, and is a key concept in the Toyota Production System (TPS) as one of the three types of waste (muda, mura, muri)
Mura	斑 Unevenness; irregularity; lack of uniformity; nonuniformity; inequality
OKR	Objectives key results Quantified and numeric objectives

P

Poka-Yoke	ポカヨケ Mistake-proofing or inadvertent error prevention
PDCA	Plan, Do, Check, Act: it is an iterative four-step management method used in business for the control and continuous improvement of processes and products

S

Seisan Hoshiki	生産方式 Method to prevent any form of waste in production
Shopfloor	Production place, operations
Supermarkets	The location where a predetermined standard inventory is kept to supply downstream processes
Taiiku	体育 Modern education integrating mental and physical education

T

TIMWOOD	7 types of waste
Tokuiku	徳育 Kuiku means to develop your rational interpersonal skills as a leader. Rational development (tokuiku) is different from logical development (chiiku)
Toyota Way	Toyota Way トヨタウェイ Centralizing the customer within the philosophy of operations

V

Value-add	Everything the customer is willing to pay
Value Stream Mapping	The value stream mapping process helps companies to create a detailed visualization of all steps in the work process. It is a representation of the flow of goods from supplier to customer through the entire value chain and organization
Visualization	Making results, gaps, processes or activities transparent, normally via a dashboard. Important tool in lean management
Waste	Anything, which will not be paid by the customer. Must be reduced or eliminated
5S	seiri (整理), seiton (整頓), seisō (清掃), seiketsu (清潔), and shitsuke (躾) Workplace method for eliminating waste and making the workplace more efficient
5 Why Analysis	Root cause analysis by asking five times why?

Index

M. Helmold, *Lean Management and Kaizen*, Management for Professionals, https://doi.org/10.1007/978-3-030-46981-8

The manufacturer's authorised representative in the EU is Springer Nature Customer Service Centre GmbH, Europaplatz 3, 69115 Heidelberg, Germany. If you have any concerns regarding our products, please contact ProductSafety@springernature.com

Printed and bound by CPI Group (UK) Ltd, Croydon, CR0 4YY

05/10/2026

02228124-0002